IN THE SHADOW OF ENOCH POWELL

Manchester University Press

Racism, Resistance and Social Change

FORTHCOMING BOOKS IN THIS SERIES

Race and riots in Thatcher's Britain: Simon Peplow

African and Mexican American men and collective violence, 1915–65: Margarita Aragon

Citizenship and belonging: Ben Gidley

In the shadow of Enoch Powell

Race, locality and resistance

Shirin Hirsch

Manchester University Press

The right of Shirin Hirsch to be identified as the author of this work has been asserted by her in accordance with the Copyright, Designs and Patents Act 1988.

Published by Manchester University Press
Altrincham Street, Manchester M1 7JA
www.manchesteruniversitypress.co.uk

British Library Cataloguing-in-Publication Data
A catalogue record for this book is available from the British Library

ISBN 978 1 5261 2739 6 paperback
ISBN 978 1 5261 2737 2 hardback

First published 2018

The publisher has no responsibility for the persistence or accuracy of URLs for any external or third-party internet websites referred to in this book, and does not guarantee that any content on such websites is, or will remain, accurate or appropriate.

Typeset by Out of House Publishing
Printed in Great Britain
by TJ International Ltd, Padstow

Contents

List of figures　　　　　　　　　　　　　　　　　　vi
Foreword by Patrick Vernon　　　　　　　　　　　vii
Series editors' foreword　　　　　　　　　　　　　x
Acknowledgements　　　　　　　　　　　　　　　　xii

Introduction　　　　　　　　　　　　　　　　　　　1

1　'The Commonwealth is much too common for me':
　another 1968　　　　　　　　　　　　　　　　　　12

2　The world in Wolverhampton　　　　　　　　　　29

3　Reverberations from 'Rivers of Blood'　　　　　　49

4　Resistance in the schools and on the buses　　　　72

5　A 'monstrous reputation': remembering Enoch Powell　92

Conclusion　　　　　　　　　　　　　　　　　　　109

Notes　　　　　　　　　　　　　　　　　　　　115
Bibliography　　　　　　　　　　　　　　　　　130
Index　　　　　　　　　　　　　　　　　　　　138

Figures

1   Protest against Enoch Powell in Wolverhampton,
late 1960s. Express & Star Newspaper Ltd.   66

2   Protest in Wolverhampton, reported on 24 April 1968.
Express & Star Newspaper Ltd.   67

3   Protest called by the Black People's Alliance outside
Rhodesia House, reported on 12 January 1969.
Express & Star Newspaper Ltd.   68

4   Protest in Wolverhampton, reported on 4 May 1968.
Express & Star Newspaper Ltd.   69

5   Protest in Wolverhampton, reported on 24 April 1968.
Express & Star Newspaper Ltd.   70

6   Vote in North Wolverhampton Working Men's Club, 22 April
1968. Express & Star Newspaper Ltd.   70

7   'Marchers supporting Mr Enoch Powell on the
Dudley Road today after leaving St Peter's gardens
bound for Dudley', reported on 27 April 1968.
Express & Star Newspaper Ltd.   71

8   Mike and Ray in West Park primary school, a
photograph disseminated by the *Sunday Jamaica Gleaner*
in the 21 April 1968 issue. ZUMA Press, Inc. /
Alamy Stock Photo.   71

Foreword

Patrick Vernon

M Y PARENTS FIRST arrived to Wolverhampton from Jamaica in the late 1950s. As part of the Windrush Generation they were invited as British subjects to help rebuild the country in the reconstruction and aftermath of the Second World War. It is seventy years on from the arrival of the HMT *Empire Windrush*, which has come to symbolise not just a generation of Caribbean migrants but also the wider post-war migration from different parts of the former British Empire to the United Kingdom. The book reflects on this history of migration, citizenship and belonging in Wolverhampton and nationally. Shirin Hirsch has been able to research and capture through oral testimony and archive material the environment and mood of the 1950s and 1960s leading up to Powell's speech and its impact in Wolverhampton.

Fifty years on, the timing of this book is critical as we reflect on the legacy of Enoch Powell's 'Rivers of Blood' speech. Sadly his speech has been used as a barometer for immigration and race relations policy for successive Labour and Conservative governments over the decades as well as inspiring the far right in the UK and across Europe. In his 1968 speech, Powell argued that Britain was 'mad' to take on an extra 50,000 dependants coming to Britain and that there should be stringent limits on black and brown people. Repatriation became Powell's political call, and he argued that if this advice was not heeded the country would enter into a racial civil war. Powell's prophecy has not come true but his calls to action were certainly brought into mainstream politics. The genealogy of the 'hostile environment' for immigrants can be traced back to Powell's words, and has been adapted by Theresa May, first as Home Secretary and now Prime Minister. In this context the Windrush Generation and their children were seen as easy targets by the government for deportation.

In 2018 these government attacks on the Windrush Generation emerged and became a national scandal. It became public knowledge that the Home Office had deported, threatened deportation or prevented the Windrush Generation and their children from re-entering Britain after visits to the Caribbean. They were deemed not British despite the 1948 British Nationality Act. The public reaction, along with the media, campaigners and some politicians, forced the government to U-turn, leading to the resignation of Amber Rudd as Home Secretary. Meanwhile the government policy has led to thousands of victims either losing their jobs, unable to access health care, losing entitlement to pensions and benefits, emotional trauma, suicide and loss of civil liberties where people have been detained and treated as criminals.

There are cases like that of Paulette Wilson from Wolverhampton who came to the UK as a ten-year-old and was on the verge of being deported back to Jamaica in 2018. This attack returned us to Powell's narrative, as human beings like Wilson were simply understood as a 'problem' that should never have been allowed to enter the UK. However, the Windrush scandal also highlighted the limits of Powellism in Britain as people have challenged the attacks on Wilson and others, both locally and nationally.

Shirin's discussion in this book of Powell's reference to education and the use of the expression 'immigrant children' resonates with me, growing up as I did in Wolverhampton during the 1960s and 1970s. I attended Grove Junior School, which Powell attended the opening of in December 1968. He treated my school, plus West Park Primary School, as a political football, treating us as second-class citizens. He articulated a vision in which 'immigrant children' would bring down education standards, especially when we were in large numbers. Apparently we would have a negative impact on white pupils' educational prospects. Most of my peers were either born in Wolverhampton or came over as minors from the Caribbean, India or East Africa (ironically there were more Polish and Italian in Wolverhampton but Powell did not see these children as a problem). Despite Powell's claims to the contrary, we were British and not immigrants!

The consequence of Powell's speech gave the education authority further incentive to treat more of us as educationally sub-normal. A lot of us were bussed around different schools outside Wolverhampton to reduce the number of black pupils and prevent white flight from local primary schools, and finally most of us were not encouraged to develop our educational abilities and thus subsequently went to failing secondary schools prior to the creation of comprehensives and left with no GCSEs. My experience of growing up in Wolverhampton, where the National Front had regular marches, was one of constant fear and the feeling of being under siege in a multicultural neighbourhood. This reminded you every day that being black and British was a struggle for acceptance and belonging.

Luckily some of us were able to fight against the odds and get a decent education and go to university, acquire decent engineering apprenticeships or clerical jobs. But I think Powell has a lot to answer for to the thousands of children of Caribbean and Asian backgrounds whose potential and future careers he blighted.

This book is an important contribution in the history of anti-racist struggle in the Midlands and nationally and it dispels the myth in many local history books of Wolverhampton and the Black Country that we were either invisible or did not fight for our rights. Finally, the book provides the perfect evidence base for the case that Powell does not deserve a blue plaque in his old constituency. There are numerous blue plaques to the great and the good of Wolverhampton but Powell is not one of them. What Wolverhampton now needs are more plaques of people from the Caribbean and Africa, but also the Polish, Italian, Sikh, Hindu and East Asian African communities who have played an important role in the public life of Wolverhampton.

Patrick Vernon is a campaigner and writer and is the founder of the 100 Great Black Britons campaign (www.100greatblackbritons.com/). He is also leading a campaign for a national Windrush day (http://windrushday.org.uk/).

Series editors' foreword

John Solomos, Satnam Virdee, Aaron Winter

THE STUDY OF race, racism and ethnicity has expanded greatly from the end of the twentieth century onwards. This expansion has coincided with a growing awareness of the continuing role that these issues play in contemporary societies all over the globe. *Racism, Resistance and Social Change* is a new series of books that seeks to make a substantial contribution to this growing field of scholarship and research. We are committed to providing a forum for the publication of the highest quality scholarship on race, racism, anti-racism and ethnic relations. As Editors of this series we would like to publish both theoretically driven books and texts with an empirical frame that seeks to further develop our understanding of the origins, development and contemporary forms of racisms, racial inequalities and racial and ethnic relations. We welcome work from a range of theoretical and political perspectives and as the series develops we would ideally want to encourage a conversation that goes beyond specific national or geopolitical environments. While we are aware that there are important differences between national and regional research traditions we hope that scholars from a variety of disciplines and multidisciplinary frames will take to opportunity to include their research work in the series.

As the title of the series highlights we would also welcome texts that can address issues about resistance and anti–racism as well as the role of political and policy interventions in this rapidly changing field. The changing forms of racist mobilisation and expression that have come to the fore in recent years have highlighted the need for more reflection and research on the role of political and civil society mobilisations in this field.

We are committed to building on theoretical advances by providing an arena for new and challenging theoretical and empirical studies on the changing morphology of race and racism in contemporary societies.

Acknowledgements

I'VE RESEARCHED AND written this book in a year when I have been employed at the University of Wolverhampton, and during this time I have been incredibly lucky to have met some of the most wonderful people who have made me feel welcome here. Huge thanks to everyone in the faculty and particularly to Pauline Anderson, Komal Chauhan, Pam Cross, Michael Cunningham, Keith Gildart, George Gosling, Shirin Housee, Grace Millar, Edda Nicholson, Paul Rae and Caroline Robinson. Outside the university it has been a privilege to work on the 'Many Rivers to Cross' exhibition at the Wolverhampton gallery with the inspiring artists/ historians Anand Chhabra, Jagdish Patel and Vanley Burke. Working with West Park primary school has been a brilliant experience with Lisa Harrison, all of the children I met at the school as well as Mike Edwards and Angela Spence from the 'class of 68'. I have also learnt a great deal from all those in Black Country Stand Up to Racism, who continue to connect theory with practice. The Wolverhampton Archives has been a vital resource as well as the *Express and Star* who have kindly allowed me to reprint a selection of their photographs. Thanks for reading drafts or helpful discussions to Jefny Ashcroft, Alice Bloch, Kambiz Boomla, Geoff Brown, Karis Campion, Tom Dark, Rosanna Farrell, Joanna Gilmore, Dharmi Kapadia, Anna Livingstone, Andrew Smith, Patrick Vernon and Paul Ward. Particular thanks to all those I interviewed and who shared their thoughts and time with me. Finally, thanks to my family, Soraya Boomla, Robin Hirsch, Rosa Hirsch, Steve Rolf, Ruby Hirsch, Kathleen Sherry, and my beautiful partner, David Swanson, for supporting me to write this book.

Introduction

O N   A   S A T U R D A Y afternoon in the spring of 1968 Enoch Powell gave a talk in a small upstairs room in Birmingham's Midland Hotel. In many ways the event seemed inconspicuous, with a Conservative shadow minister speaking to roughly eighty-five Tories. The speech was not directed towards these individuals alone, however. Intent on reaching a mass audience, Powell had delivered advanced transcripts to the national and local press, and the Birmingham-based company ATV sent a television crew that captured the partial clips of the speech that survive. Powell's prophecy on racial warfare and blood-foaming rivers reverberated across the country. A ferocious attack on black immigration was unleashed.

To bring this enemy to life, Powell let it be known that he had recently fallen into conversation with a constituent, a 'middle-aged, quite ordinary working man employed in one of our nationalised industries'. The man, Powell explained, was desperate to leave his own country for fear of the increasing immigrant numbers. Yet the words of this 'decent, ordinary fellow Englishman' began to blur into the words of Powell. 'In this country in 15 or 20 years time, the black man will have the whip hand over the white man' said Powell, or the man, or perhaps they had become one and the same by this point. Throughout the speech Powell presented himself as the voice of these white Wolverhampton people, speaking for and through the crafted characters of his constituency, their words now articulated in the ventriloquism of Powell's public voice. In contrast, immigrants entered the narrative as voiceless, threatening figures, removed from any sense of decency. In Wolverhampton these immigrants had supposedly been breeding rapidly, spreading noise and confusion, breaking windows and pushing excreta through the letter boxes of white residents. The immigrant children, 'charming wide grinning piccaninnies', were known to terrorise elderly white women for enjoyment; they knew no other English except the word 'racialist' which they eagerly chanted. Against the background of Martin Luther King's assassination and black risings in the United States, Powell ended with a prophecy that came to informally entitle the speech: 'As I look ahead, I am filled with foreboding, like the Roman, I seem to see the River Tiber foaming with much blood.' Fusing classical imagery and the anecdotes of the nameless ordinary 'little man', the 'Rivers of Blood' speech would define Enoch Powell's career.[1]

The response was immediate. Just as Powell had planned, his words secured front-page news and national attention. The following day Powell was sacked from the shadow cabinet for a speech that the Conservative leader Heath described as 'racialist in tone' and which was clearly an attempt to seize control of the party.[2] Support continued, however, and Powell received thousands of letters of admiration, to such an extent that the Wolverhampton sorting office was apparently unable to cope with the levels of post arriving for him.[3] Meanwhile small groups of workers across the country demonstrated public support for the Conservative politician through strike action and protests. A Gallup opinion poll at the end of April suggested that 74 per cent of the British electorate agreed with Powell's sentiments as expressed in the speech, and showed that he was the favourite candidate to become the next Conservative leader.[4] Crossman, then leader of the House of Commons, wrote in his diary on 27 April that Powell had 'stirred up the nearest thing to a mass movement since the 1930s ... Enoch is stimulating the real revolt of the masses ... he has changed the whole shape of politics overnight'.[5] For a fleeting moment the speech seemed able to capture the support of large sections of the British population.

This book is concerned with how the industrial town of Wolverhampton was drawn into this new focus, as Powell's gaze moved from the global to the local.[6] Powell was the MP for Wolverhampton South West and had based his speech within the anecdotal imaginings of the town's streets, schools, buses and people. The town was presented by Powell as a microcosm of England in its ordinariness, as well as a neglected and forgotten contrast to much of the country. The research here provides a closer reading of this local focus, contributing to the literature on Powell and our understanding of race, class and resistance during a critical moment in British society. It is the purpose of this book to more seriously understand the relationship between Powell and those he claimed to represent as well as oppose.

That Powell often claimed to be speaking on behalf of his white constituents has been repeated in much of the somewhat hagiographic literature on Powell. The 'Rivers of Blood' speech is presented as the honest reporting from Powell's perspective as MP where immigration was causing 'growing concerns' within his constituency.[7] The research here challenges this direct relationship with Powell as spokesman for the people. For one thing, the town was also represented by another two MPs, both Labour politicians who spoke out strongly against Powell's speech. Moreover, Powell's preoccupation with the local was entirely new to his politics in 1968. In his turn to a new anti-immigrant politics, Wolverhampton provided a concrete focus through which a renegotiation of race could be born, away from the global heights of Empire.

This sudden geographical turn needs further examination. The recent work of Camilla Schofield allows us to grasp this trajectory on a national and global scale, impressively situating the politics of Powell within the rise and fall of the British Empire. For Schofield, Powell was deeply touched by the lessons of Empire's end through which the black immigrant came to embody imperial decline. Yet within this argument, Powell followed a particular English path with a certain coherence to it.[8] In contrast, this research stresses the dramatic shift in Powell's politics through which his constituency became a new concern. Paul Foot's early classic on the resistible rise of Powell is important in framing this analysis, a work that first exposed a political transformation in Powell's new focus on immigration. As decolonisation spread across the globe, Powell's politics abruptly shifted from Empire enthusiast to little Englander and for Foot, the 'Rivers of Blood' speech was marked by opportunistic hypocrisy.[9]

There has been significant new research on reformulations of race at this critical moment in British history, just as the post-war consensus began to crumble.[10] This book builds on this work, examining the ways in which new economic uncertainties opened up unusual and tentative political formations for Powell. To further understand these new openings, this book investigates Powell's spatial fixation and the ways in which his words were translated into his constituency in Wolverhampton.

Discovering Wolverhampton

This local focus was not unique and, in the aftermath of the 'Rivers of Blood' speech, Wolverhampton was pulled into the national spotlight. It served as a tantalising symbol of the heart of the nation, providing a magnifying glass on subterranean national politics. The town soon found itself an attractive site for media expeditions, with numerous media accounts of Powell's constituency produced on the 'well known' racial tensions of the area. Wolverhampton came to be directly associated with Powell's anti-immigrant position within this reporting, to such an extent that it was described simply as 'Powell country' by one national journalist.[11] This newfound curiosity meant that journalists were suddenly concerned to hear the opinions of residents from a town that had rarely featured until then. Two weeks after the speech, for example, Wolverhampton was the subject of a national radio programme and individuals in a local pub were directly questioned on whether they would like a 'coloured man' living next to them. 'I would go raving mad' responded a local drinker.[12] A week later, Wolverhampton hosted 'a party of foreign journalists' from the Foreign Press Association to examine the reality of the 'immigration situation' in the area. Based on a six-hour tour of the town, the findings were drawn up and it was concluded that the 'colour problem' in Wolverhampton was 'hiding under a dark cloud'.[13] The *Observer*, keen to demonstrate its knowledge of the town, went so far as to produce a visual map of where 'coloured people' lived in Wolverhampton. The coding for the map was outlined with a gradation of colours; the darker the colour the more 'coloured people' there were occupying an area of the town.[14]

Similarly, the *Times* became suddenly attentive to the Black Country and published a special issue on the area in 1968, spurred on by Powell's speech. One article, entitled 'Dark Question Mark', assured readers that as a rich town Wolverhampton was far from the 'grimy Black Country wilderness that it looks from a comfortable window seat'. The town could boast the largest Woolworths in Europe, and within the Mander shopping centre, a 'multi-million pound monument', even the shops were carpeted. Yet despite the economic prosperity of the town, the article concluded that 'with this continued influx from overseas there is a real fear that this part of the Black Country will become even blacker, and that the imaginative possibility exists one day of the area becoming synonymous with the American south'. The local anxiety, 'not just of the prejudiced but of the worried', was based on the assumption that the indigenous population would move out and the immigrants would move in so that 'fears of an eventual blacker and blacker Wolverhampton multiply'.[15] In the 1969 BBC documentary 'Strangers in a Town', the industrial transformation of Wolverhampton was also depicted in connection with the 'problems' of immigration. The narrator explained to viewers that on the top of a hill in the middle of England lay a town of 265,000 people. The discovery of the town following Powell's speech thus produced lengthy musings on the 'odd case of Wolverhampton'.[16] The town quickly became a reified symbol of the newly constructed 'colour problem', providing a curious provincial backdrop to frame the debates initiated by Powell.

Needless to say these contemporary accounts were not attentive to the complex but also overlapping relations that were developing within the town. Most evidently, the superficial reports of the town often rendered black people silent, merely a subject for others to discuss. The few times when Commonwealth immigrants are questioned and we hear their voices, it is difficult to garner any real understanding of their thoughts and feelings, since they are represented only as a burden or an outsider subject. For example, soon after the 'Rivers of Blood' speech Enoch Powell made new proposals to pay for fares 'home' for immigrants. This was reported on by Midlands News TV through a vox pop with anyone assumed to be a black immigrant stopped and interrogated on whether they would return to their country of birth if their fare was paid by the government. The questioning, with its threatening undertones, left those singled out for the news report forced to give uncomfortable answers on the strength of their settlement in Britain. One Caribbean man responded that he was happy in Britain, but 'if they want to get rid of me well I'll go'.[17] Such reporting framed those black interviewees not as residents with rights, but as a problem that needed to be dealt with.

Even so, these media accounts do reveal the heightened atmosphere following the speech in which black people found themselves under intense scrutiny. In this vein, accounts written by black British authors often stress the significance of the 'Rivers of Blood' speech as a key moment in questions of belonging, race and the nation. Stuart Hall recalled:

> I had recently moved to Birmingham and will never forget the impact of the 'Rivers of Blood' speech. I remember the sudden, shared feeling of fear, the sense of hostility, the huddling together against the impending violence, the unspoken aggression in the streets as little groups of black men and women came together to discuss how to respond to the violence it seemed calculated to unleash. There were already reserves of resentment in places like Birmingham, Coventry and the Black Country against the post war tide of immigrants looking for jobs. Now the dyke had burst, the taboos were broken: and we felt suddenly adrift and unprotected in an alien country.[18]

Similarly, Mike Phillips wrote that the memory of Enoch Powell 'will probably have me looking over my shoulder in the streets of my own city, London, for the rest of my life … I shall always think of him as part of my history and as part of my identity'.[19] This impact was felt perhaps most strongly by black people living in Wolverhampton, with recollections of feeling 'under siege'. Vanessa Kirkpatrick was an eleven-year-old girl in the constituency of Wolverhampton North East when Powell made his 'Rivers of Blood' speech. 'I can still remember vividly the fear I felt as a young black girl' she explains. 'I recall being unable to sleep the night that

Powell expressed his inflammatory views ... I feared going to school the next day – where I was just one of around half a dozen black pupils. Maybe it was the over active imagination of a young child, but I actually thought I might be lynched.'[20] The polarisation which emerged following Powell's speech seemed to exist in concentrated form in Wolverhampton.

Despite this reality, black people are often written out of the speech and the town's history. A journalist sent to Wolverhampton in 1968 observed that the official handbook of the town appeared to completely ignore the presence of 'coloured people' with neither the pictorial matter nor the copy making any reference to them. The journalist noted that this was a 'peculiar situation' when Wolverhampton was home to 'fourteen and a half thousand coloured citizens' that had recently been the focus of Britain's race relations debate.[21] This has been repeated in accounts of the town ever since. In nostalgic histories such as *Wolverhampton Memories* the photographs show only white residents. When immigration is mentioned at all it is in relation to a 'Latin love and romance' between an Italian migrant and a Wolverhampton local.[22] The published photographs of Wolverhampton's history show scenes of all-white dances in the 1950s and 1960s; the absence of black people is neither noted nor explained.[23]

In contrast, this book draws out a history of black people in the town that has previously been ignored, tracing the racialised divisions which had existed and were strengthened in this period. This was not a natural phenomenon but a process in which race had to be constantly made and remade. In this sense, the book reveals how particular residents within the town came to think of themselves as white or black. Yet the research also documents how, beneath the surface, new forms of living had also emerged within the town, illuminating the contradictory ways in which new immigrants lived and worked with those already residing in the town.

Methods

In examining this history, the research draws from interviews with those who lived through this speech in Wolverhampton, using interviews undertaken by the author as well as using the rich resource of the BEME collection with black and ethnic minority residents of Wolverhampton at the start of the twenty-first century. In addition, Powell's speech transcripts, parliamentary records, national and local media reports as well as private and public archival material are all used. The newspapers, in particular, were significant in the story of Powell's speech, with Powell intent on achieving maximum media coverage. Powell had already made a speech in Walsall in February of 1968 with all of the same themes of his 'Rivers of Blood' speech yet it had received little attention. Powell's April speech in Birmingham was, in this respect, a huge success. By Sunday it was the lead story in every newspaper.[24]

Of course, media reports were by no means neutral and while readers were not simply 'subject' to media reporting, the newspaper played an important, albeit critically absorbed, role in framing the speech. As early as 1870, Marx noted that the racial antagonisms between Irish and English workers were kept artificially alive and intensified by the press.[25] Du Bois too wrote of the Jim Crow era in the American South and the role of newspapers in specialising in reports that flattered poor whites while almost utterly ignoring black people except in stories of crime and as objects of ridicule.[26] Engaging with material realities and everyday experiences, newspapers can name, map and define a town in specific ways.[27]

The two local papers in Wolverhampton, the daily *Express and Star* and the weekly *Wolverhampton Chronicle*, were no different in this respect. With an average daily circulation of roughly a quarter of a million throughout the 1960s, the *Express and Star* was crucial in forming and articulating a racialised 'local community', providing a sense of familiarity with the area and an expression of a known, Wolverhampton identity.[28] During the 'Rivers of Blood' speech, the *Express and Star* seized the opportunity to report on the issue locally with extensive coverage in the weeks that followed. The day after the speech, the front page was simply a reprint of Powell's words, with a call for readers to write in to the paper to show either support or opposition, and thousands of local readers responded with overwhelming support for Powell's speech.[29] This editorial framing was also highly contested. A week after the speech a demonstration was organised against Powell by local students from the Wulfrun College of

Further Education, as well as the Wolverhampton Technical Teachers College. The *Express and Star* offices became a key site within the protest route. A letter delivered to the newspaper read: 'we protest at the role of your newspaper in encouraging the expression of racial prejudice now rife in this town. Since the time that immigrants arrived in this town you have used news items in such a way as to present immigrants in the worst light.' During the week of the speech, the protestors argued the newspaper had 'acted with almost criminal irresponsibility in conducting a ballot which invited every racially prejudiced person in the area to make clear their racial prejudice'. The letter was signed from 'the workers, students and immigrants of Wolverhampton'.[30] Similarly, following local council elections in the area soon after the speech a defeated candidate, ex Labour councillor Arthur Morey of Wednesfield North West, criticised the newspaper for 'playing up' the immigration issue night after night. 'Without the aid of the *Express and Star* this election would have been completely different' he argued.[31] Much of the literature on Powell portrays the then editor of the local newspaper as something of a hero, standing up for his own editorial principles against the racist tone of Powell's speech. The editor maintained a close friendship with Powell up until the delivery of the speech and provided extensive media advice on achieving the utmost coverage, advice which was clearly heeded by the MP.[32] Following the national reaction to the speech, the editorial supported Heath's sacking of Powell from the shadow cabinet, and agreed that the tone of the speech had been 'unnecessarily extravagant', but they also argued that for too long there had been a neglect from those in authority to the 'problems' of immigration, with the notable exception of their own newspaper.[33] Indeed, Powell's new intervention was described acerbically as his 'quite belated emergence in the Messianic role'.[34] Instead of an intrepid outburst from Powell, key parts of his speech had already emerged within the local paper.

The local newspapers are thus an important resource within this research but were not neutral bystanders. The contemporary sources drawn from in this book frequently reveal – sometimes inadvertently and sometimes explicitly – racial prejudices that were dominant at the time. This is particularly obvious with the common use of the term 'coloured' to refer to black people. This book uses this term only when quoting these sources and for the rest of the book instead uses the political terminology of black to describe those with heritage from the Caribbean and Indian subcontinent.

Chapter 1 of this book explores these black experiences in Britain and how they related to dramatic global changes as well as national shifts in relation to race, class and resistance. Enoch Powell and his 'Rivers of Blood' speech are situated within the reverberations of 1968, and the chapter examines the ways in which common global underlying processes expressed themselves in very different national forms. Just as global protests were spreading, Powell displayed a newfound concern with his local constituency. Chapter 2 argues that beneath the surface, however, more complex dynamics existed in Wolverhampton in which race was both a real force and also undermined by everyday relations. These tensions are further discussed through a longer history of the town. Chapter 3 centres on the immediate impact of the speech in both national and local settings and interrogates the opposing responses Powell's words provoked. Chapter 4 focuses on everyday resistance to racism that was simmering within the town, examining social relations on both the local buses and in the schools. Powell drew these two disputes into a national debate as a way of strengthening racial divisions. Yet the resistance on the buses and in the schools also highlighted an emerging anti-racist movement that, while still unorganised in this period, would begin to develop into an explicit opposition in the years that followed. Finally, in chapter 5 the memories of Powell and his speech are examined. This chapter looks at the ways in which the speech has since been remembered, by powerful forces on a national scale as well as more local responses within the multicultural city of Wolverhampton. The shadow of Powell remains significant within British politics. Yet it is a shadow which exists within particular boundaries and there is a continual battle over Powell's legacy. A rooted anti-racist tradition has restrained a direct and open rehabilitation of the politician.

This book is therefore about Powell and his speech, but more importantly it is about the agency of ordinary people, both black and white, who were suddenly thrown into a national debate and responded in different ways. Powell's 'Rivers of Blood' speech broke through an oscillation between the visible and the hidden that had been building throughout the decade. The national words of this Conservative figure revealed a racism that had already existed on a local scale, yet was now given new form to enable its survival within a rapidly changing Britain. As Britain's empire began to crumble, the industrial town of Wolverhampton found itself the site through which a new 'immigrant' enemy was both defined and targeted. The resistance to Powell's words in 1968 was a minority action, and yet it would lay the foundations in which, over the next decade, a multiracial working class was forged through anti-racist movements.[35] To understand these convulsions, it is to this revolutionary year of 1968 that the book now turns.

1

'The Commonwealth is much too common for me': another 1968

IN JUNE 1967 the first live, international satellite television programme, 'Our World', was broadcast to the largest television audience ever up to that date, with an estimated 400 million viewers in twenty-four countries. The show closed with a live performance from the Beatles written especially for the broadcast. In the middle of a dreamlike set, the band sang 'All You Need is Love' surrounded by balloons, flowers and multilingual placards. At the height of the Vietnam War, the idealistic words appeared to capture the oppositional sentiments of the 'Summer of Love'. The track went on to top the charts. Nine months after the broadcast, however, Powell's publicised speech served as a powerful rejection of this counterculture. For Powell, love was certainly not all you needed. Even so, the two moments were not completely separate. In the 'Our World' broadcast the Beatles had invited many of their musician friends to sing along with the chorus, including Eric Clapton, members of the Rolling Stones and Marianne Faithfull. In 1976 Clapton went on to declare his support for Enoch Powell as part of an angry tirade at his own concert. 'Enoch for Prime Minister', Clapton shouted, and then repeated the slogan the National Front had popularised to 'Keep Britain White'.[1] In under a decade, love had transformed into explicit racism. For the Beatles, Powell's words also reverberated. In the improvised yet never released track 'Commonwealth Song' the Beatles satirised the speech, mocking 'dirty Enoch Powell' and his travels around the British Empire;

John Lennon, in the voice of a prim old English woman, sings 'The Commonwealth is much too common for me'. The song went through several versions before 'Get Back' was officially released in 1969 as a commentary on counterculture.[2]

This chapter situates Powell's 'Rivers of Blood' speech within a global period of dramatic changes, a movement described by Sartre as a radical contestation of every established value in society. 1968 was a year marked by the Vietnam War and victory for the Viet Cong. The Black Panthers were powerfully challenging the racism of the American state while in Paris students and workers were in revolt. Peaceful and violent decolonisation spread across the globe and in Czechoslovakia the Soviet Union sent in tanks to crush a rebellion. The turmoil of the old order became dramatically apparent as certainties of the past were confronted.[3] Powell's role within this period, and particularly his 'Rivers of Blood' speech, was not obviously located within these changes. In 1965, Powell had described himself as 'not a revolutionary or rebel or anything like that', but a 'party man – a professional Tory'. He claimed not to be bothered about crazes – 'I've got nothing against the Beatles' – or about fashion – 'I shall continue to wear a waistcoat to the end of my days'. Instead he argued he was a conventional man and would stick to conventional politics.[4] The conservatism of Powell would however break free from party discipline when in 1968 he made a speech that went far beyond the restrained language of his party leadership. Powell's outburst was both informed by and rejected the eruptions of 1968 and this chapter explores the speech within the deeper transformations of this critical year. To understand the purchase of Powell's words at this specific moment, the chapter now turns to the post-war period and the sense of stability that permeated many aspects of life. Experiences of this period would be significant in framing Powell's speech when, in the late 1960s, all that was solid melted into air.

Boom, migration and the long calm

In the post-war period capitalism experienced the longest boom in its history. Mirroring this global trend, Britain was marked by political consensus, trade union partnerships and affluence for many.[5] The apparent calm of the country was expressed by a number of thinkers from across the political spectrum celebrating a newfound harmony within the capitalist system. In fact, the Labour Party figure Crosland went so far as to argue that 'by 1951 Britain had, in all essentials, ceased to be a capitalist country'.[6] Crosland was certainly not alone in his thinking and such optimism continued throughout the decade. Four years later Crosland wrote that contemporary society would have seemed 'like a paradise' to many early socialist pioneers. Poverty and insecurity were in the process of disappearing as Britain stood 'on the threshold of mass abundance'.[7] Abundance, however, was predicated on a historical relationship which ensured the dependency of the colonial periphery on the centre. This prolonged entanglement was often written out of the national story of Britain, and yet it was a global system that deeply shaped Enoch Powell.

Since childhood, Powell had been wedded to an idea of the nation framed through imperial power. Englishness for Powell was a set of values and a state of mind, and transmitting these great ideals abroad had been his romantic vision of Empire. Such a position was aligned with Conservative ideology in this period, and Powell was, in his own words, 'born a Tory'. From a middle-class family Powell followed all the traits of a typical Conservative path. Grammar school led to a place at Cambridge to study classics, and then a stint as a professor in Australia. He had grown up with a strong loyalty to imperial Britain, but it was his experience of the Second World War that developed this passion for Empire as he cut his career in academia short and enlisted into the army. Rising up the ranks of the military and removed from combat, his time in India allowed Powell's love of Empire to truly blossom, seeing first-hand what he romantically described as the 'spell of England' projected onto the islands 'under influence'.[8] Empire, for Powell, was a world system deeply enshrined in his very being, interwoven into what it meant to be an Englishman. When the war ended, Powell harboured dreams of returning to colonial India in the role of viceroy. One way to protect the Empire, Powell calculated, was a career in politics. His love of Empire and capitalism were not unique for a Conservative parliamentary candidate, and neither was his election in 1950, as MP for Wolverhampton South West, particularly surprising. Powell's early life seemed to represent a success story of middle-class aspiration and English conservatism.

Powell's election as MP was framed by the post-war boom. It was also a time when industry was met with serious labour shortages in Britain. The king's speech on the opening of parliament in 1951, the first written by a Tory government since the war had ended, declared 'My government views with concern the serious shortage of labour, particularly of skilled labour, which has handicapped production in a number of industries'.[9] Responding to this gap, the government at first focused on the recruitment of white migrants, in an attempt to preserve an imagined white Britain. Nevertheless, migrant numbers from Europe were not sufficient to satisfy the labour-hungry demands of British industry. For a short time it looked as though the British economy would be throttled by a shortage of labour. What saved it was, in Foot's words, the historical accident of imperialism.[10] Drawing from the resources of the Commonwealth, immigrants from the Caribbean and the Indian subcontinent would have to be recruited to Britain.

There had been black communities of sorts in Britain since the 1500s and immigration to Britain in the post-war period was by no means a new phenomenon.[11] Over the 1950s there was something of a migrant labour boom, but this did not solely include those classified as 'coloured immigrants'. The numbers of migrants arriving in Britain from Poland, for example, was actually equivalent to their Caribbean counterparts in 1960.[12] Of course, it was the migration of people from the Caribbean and India that received the most attention in this period. Their skin marked them out as internal Others within the nation; they were *in* Britain but not *of* Britain.[13] These racial hierarchies were framed by a history of British colonialism, where the imagined role of white Britain was presented as that of protecting and overseeing the people, infrastructure and land of darkened colonies. The arrival to British shores of those from the colonies, now legally as equals, was therefore a direct challenge to a racial ideology entrenched within British colonialism.

Simultaneously, however, the rules of Empire also pushed against immigration restrictions within the Commonwealth. Empire had created subjects of the crown and to conceptually reject this also meant threatening the very workings of the system. Speaking some years later, Sir David Hunt, Winston Churchill's Private Secretary, paraphrased the dilemma thus: 'The minute we said we've got to keep these black chaps out, the whole Commonwealth lark would have blown up.'[14] Moreover, recent popular memories of the British war effort were centred on defeating the Nazis and their ideology of racial purity. In this sense a new political campaign against 'coloured' immigration was hard to sell to the British public in the years following the war.

At first the numbers of new black immigrants arriving in Britain was relatively small: no more than 2,000 in any one year between 1948 (when the *Empire Windrush* brought the first arrivals) and 1953. After this date there was a qualitative change and black immigration could be measured in tens of thousands per year. This change was in part because some employers made special efforts to recruit in the Caribbean and India, with travel fares loaned which would be paid back gradually out of salaries earned in Britain. Recruiting industries included the National Health Service, of particular interest to readers here as it was then under the direction of Enoch Powell as minister of health.[15] Indeed, for Powell during this period his close attachment to Empire was still tied up with a commitment to a notion of British subjects. In other words, those living within the Commonwealth had a right to migrate to Britain.

All of these workers who arrived from the Commonwealth into Britain were not only permitted to migrate but were significantly encouraged to do so. The 1948 Nationality Act had granted citizenship to residents of Britain's colonies and former colonies and their passports gave them the right to come to Britain and stay for the rest of their lives.[16] Those from the colonies had been brought up with ideas of a superior, wealthy motherland and British life was often imagined with great optimism by future migrants in the Commonwealth. Unfortunately, these hopes did not always materialise and, on arrival, newcomers experienced racism, housing difficulties and underemployment.[17] Meanwhile there was a muted acceptance by national politicians of immigrants and their presence was acknowledged as a fact of life. While there were political voices who campaigned against 'coloured migrants', it was nevertheless a minority pursuit in the 1950s and early 1960s. Powell was certainly not part of any anti-immigrant campaign in this period. As late as 1964, Powell was arguing that the only long-term route to happiness in his constituency involved a gradual integration process of immigrant communities. Powell wrote that: 'I have set and I always will set my face like flint against making any difference between one citizen and another on grounds of his origin.'[18] This position was no different to the vast majority of politicians in this period, as Powell stressed, arguing that the overwhelming majority of Conservatives would agree with him that integration of immigrants into British life was the most desirable option. The framing of immigrants as an undesirable burden on the nation, something that must be halted, was not part of Powell's language at this stage. This could be explained by the simple reason that British capitalism had become increasingly reliant on black migrant labour. Up to and including the 1959 election, which the Conservatives won, immigration was nowhere to be seen as a mainstream political issue. The economic boom had protected black new-comer migrants from national attention and instead such migrants often kept their heads down, working hard to build a new life for themselves in Britain. As Stuart Hall put it, they were 'tiptoeing through the tulips'.[19]

Race and the end of consensus

Beneath the surface of this long calm, molecular shifts pointed to future instabilities. In the early 1960s the boom of the British economy began to very gradually come to an end. Immigrant workers were still needed, but with not quite the same urgency and scale that had determined the labour market of the 1950s. The position of racialised migrant workers became increasingly fragile within this new context. 1962 was a major turning point in the state implementation of immigration controls. Restrictions were introduced by the Conservative government on the admission of Commonwealth settlers, permitting only those with government-issued employment vouchers to settle. The leader of the Labour opposition in parliament, Hugh Gaitskell, strongly rejected the Commonwealth

Immigrants Act, describing it as 'cruel and brutal anti-colour legislation'. Blackness became equated, officially, with second-class citizenship and with the status of undesirable immigrant.[20] The discriminatory legislation, whose obvious intention was to reduce the total annual inflow of black people in Britain, sowed the seeds for future restrictions.

Two years after the Act the Conservative candidate Peter Griffiths unexpectedly won the seat of Smethwick, in the West Midlands, in the 1964 general election, fought on an openly racist platform. 'If you want a nigger for a neighbour vote Labour' read the slogan on leaflets in support of Griffiths. This local Conservative victory stood at odds with a national swing to Labour. The Smethwick result therefore seemed to demonstrate that race and immigration were potential issues that could win votes.[21] Powell observed the result in his backyard with cautious interest but remained notably quiet on the issue. Lessons from Smethwick were nevertheless drawn across the political spectrum. While Labour had strongly opposed the 1962 Act, in government its position changed. In 1965 it issued a White Paper on Immigration from the Commonwealth, which argued that the essence of the 'problem' was numbers. Immigration controls were further tightened, with a particular focus on restrictions on the entry of black people. In March 1968 Labour initiated the passing of a new Commonwealth Immigration Act, introduced with the sole purpose of restricting the entry of Kenyan Asians holding British passports. A special clause in the act gave ex-colonials with white skin the continued right of free entry. This was a transformation within the Labour Party that was honestly acknowledged by Crossman. He wrote that 'a few years ago everyone would have regarded the denial of entry to British nationals with British passports as the most appalling violation of our deepest principles'. Crossman went on to justify this position, explaining that he supported the bill 'mainly because I am an MP for a constituency in the Midlands, where racialism is a powerful force'.[22] But in so doing, the government also increased the social and political consequences of racism, both in the Midlands and nationally. In Sivanandan's words, racism was given the sanction of the state and was made 'respectable and clinical by institutionalising it'.[23] It was in this context that Powell made his speech the following month. The passing of the Commonwealth Immigration Act, with cross-party support, gave Powell the confidence to raise the stakes. With the increased racism spurred on by Powell came yet further controls. As Paul Foot argued: 'the tiger of racialism, once unleashed, knows no master. It devours its liberators and its prey with equal ferocity'.[24]

The centre shakes

At the same time, different global trends were pulling against the reactionary racism emerging in Britain. In late 1964 in Berkeley a wave of campus revolts were initiated. They quickly spread across the world, illuminating feelings of unrest in wider society. In Britain it was observed that the scale of resistance nationally had not matched the levels of America or France. There were student occupations in Britain, of which the London School of Economics occupation was the most famous, and anti-Vietnam protests were lively and militant but restricted mainly to student networks. Meanwhile the economy was slowing and established partnerships with trade unions were being challenged by a Wilson-led Labour government. A strike by seafarers, for example, was stopped when the government called in the navy and announced a state of emergency. Widespread political disillusionment took hold within sections of the working class towards a political class that now seemed more detached from voters. While Labour continued in government, its support weakened. In the Dudley by-election of March 1968, a Labour stronghold near to Wolverhampton, an 11,000 majority for Labour disappeared as Conservatives won the seat.[25] The political centre seemed to tentatively shake.

Within the workplace things were also changing. For those who had been brought up listening to the Beatles and in a world of full employment, the late 1960s provoked new feelings of disquiet. In the same year as the release of 'Get Back' in 1969, a sociological study took place at a new Ford car plant in Liverpool. Spending time with trade union activists among the workforce, Beynon observed how these workers were united by their youth and by having 'little respect for authority'. While they still accepted tradition they seemed to be 'less bound by it' compared to an older generation of trade unionists.[26] In the late 1960s the teenagers of the previous decade became militant campaigners in Britain's factories as their working conditions were threatened. As Todd shows, these workers instigated the most radical wave of industrial unrest that the country had experienced since the 1920s. Between 1965 and 1975 Britain experienced, on average, 2,885 strikes each year. The strikes testified to a new assertiveness, provoked by the chasm between their high expectations of life in an affluent society, and the reality they experienced on the factory floor.[27]

It was in this period that Powell developed an intense disillusionment with the realities of the British Empire as he bitterly observed its dramatic decline. This had followed a gradual demoralisation which had begun to take pace following the Suez Crisis of 1956, alongside a wave of anti-colonial struggles.[28] Once a jewel to be protected with every fibre of his body, the Empire, 'that power and that glory', had now 'vanished' for Powell and he turned abruptly against his past fixation.[29] In particular, Powell found it particularly galling to watch successive British governments responding to the advancement of American dominance. He could never forgive the Conservative leader Macmillan's decision of voluntary subordination to the United States, dignified as a 'Special Relationship'.[30]

In 1965 Powell suffered a public defeat, losing the leadership of the Conservative Party to Edward Heath. Powell achieved only a distant third place in this internal election and was given the role of shadow defence minister. To stand any serious possibility of leading the party and the country, something dramatic had to change in Powell's appeal. His politics were already associated with a free-market approach, making converts among young Tories wanting to break away from the 'semi-socialist web woven by expediency in three Tory administrations' and reviving in older Tories a hope that Conservatism could again be what they had always thought it was: economically liberal.[31] Powell did not miss an opportunity to advocate his unshakeable belief in the power of capitalism. Talking of starvation in underdeveloped countries, for example, Powell argued that the best gift the West could bestow was not charity or aid, but capitalism.[32] Such a belief in capitalism and the free market was, however, not sufficient to develop the reach and power of Powell. As the *Times* noted, while

Powell's theoretical contributions to the political debate were important, they were not electorally seductive, particularly in the 'austere garments' he presented them in.[33] Powell was well aware of this impression following the failures of his leadership bid and made a sharp transition in his political focus. In an interview given just two weeks before his 'Rivers of Blood' speech, and published months later, he acknowledged: 'I deliberately include at least one startling assertion in every speech in order to attract enough attention to give me a power base within the Conservative Party.'[34]

Powell's shift towards a new anti-immigrant politics was made within this context of individual ambition as well as national crisis. In the late 1960s British capitalism was forced to cut real living standards, begin to increase unemployment and raise rents and prices. David Widgery recalled how a real fear had begun to spread within ruling class circles that the rule of law was no longer guaranteed now that the mass complacency of the 1950s and early 1960s had dissipated.[35] Powell's speech was born out of this class conflict. He devised his new political direction as a way of speaking to these problems, engaging both with the fears of the elite and those within working-class communities. It was the support from the latter grouping which was so surprising. Powell's relationship with a segment of workers was in part aided by a prevalence of racist ideas inculcated by centuries of imperialism. Yet Britain's imperial legacy was not in itself an adequate explanation. For Powell's new racism to resonate with working-class lives, his words had also to speak to the fears and disillusionment with established politics which had emerged in 1968, connecting with new material anxieties within sections of the working class who had lost faith in the succession of leaders who had betrayed their trust. In this sense, a new racial formation needed to be outlined, one in which a vision of the white race was not associated with king and Empire anymore, but instead with ordinary people.[36] As Bill Schwarz notes, the white race was re-imagined by Powell during a period of decolonisation; for Powell, to be white was now not poised in relation to the victory and strength of the ruling Empire, but instead in association with decline, victimhood and enemy occupation.[37] Similarly, Hall wrote of 1968 in Britain that as the fissures of social dissent opened, race became a theme capable of carrying forward intense, but subterranean, public emotions on a wave of reaction.[38]

In this sense, Powell offered both a superficial confrontation with the establishment and a focus on a new black threat. His words were carefully directed towards a newly constructed white working-class identity in association with employers, both reflecting and creating new divisions within the British workplace. The 'people' that Powell supportively invoked were tied into concomitant ideas of nationhood and race. With his class biography from professor in Greek to brigadier and now Conservative politician, Powell had an impressive ability to tie a new racial invocation into a defence of ordinary commonality. At a public meeting in a grammar school in Nottingham in May 1968, Powell described his relationship with workers as 'natural' at a time of crisis and argued that both trade unionists and employers were victims of the failures of a Labour government.[39] In contrast, the immigrants of the Commonwealth were excluded from any such imagined class unity. Entering a political vacuum, Powell crystallised a new enemy which had not been needed within the mainstream politics of the 1950s and early 1960s. In his Walsall speech, for example, Powell identified himself with those urban whites who resented the change in their communities. Providing a dress rehearsal for his 'Rivers of Blood' speech two months later, Powell captured working-class feelings of powerlessness and neglect:

> There is a sense of hopelessness and helplessness which comes over persons who are trapped or imprisoned, when all their efforts to attract attention and assistance bring no response. This is the kind of feeling which you in Walsall and we in Wolverhampton are experiencing in the face of the continued flow of immigration into our towns.[40]

Explaining that 'we are of course in a minority' since 'perhaps fewer than sixty constituencies were affected out of the total of 600', Powell commented that 'the rest know little or nothing and we might sometimes be tempted to feel, care little or nothing'. This was a particular identity rooted in place, of besieged towns in opposition to the 'metropolitan elite' of London. But it was also a politics that attempted to draw from particular class experiences while in the process reconciling such differences. Powell raged against the Labour government and its incompetence, in persuading 'each class in the community that the other is to blame'. The 'community' was key for Powell here, a racialised notion of the nation that attempted to resolves the tensions between classes. To do so, Powell attacked the economists, the newspapers, the political parties and especially the party which had been regarded as the workers' 'own'. All of these groups were 'at them day after day declaring that they, the workers, the men in the street, are to blame for inflation by doing too little and asking too much'. And while everybody around them seemed to accept this position, Powell noted wryly that the 'common sense of the people tells them that it is not so'. He went on to denounce the blame being laid on the workers for the problems within the economy, noting:

> A dangerous situation builds up when an accusation which they feel in their bones to be false is fastened upon whole classes of men and women, indeed upon a whole people. They become resentful, and not without reason, feeling that everyone is leagued in a conspiracy against them to pretend that black is white and innocent is guilty … The whole atmosphere of industrial relations, the whole attitude of the citizen to his country and its future has been poisoned for years by this unanimous determination of the vocal organs of opinion to pin the blame for our financial and economic ills where it does not and cannot belong.[41]

It was this 'indignation of ordinary people' that Powell was able to speak to, pulling in unusual support for the Conservative MP. On May Day protests in London 1968 there were 'angry scenes' between dockers supporting Powell and left-wing students, illuminating a clash between the new student Left and a traditional sector of the working class.[42] Just a few days later students revolted in Paris and were followed by a mass general strike of French workers. The radicalism of the workers was anxiously observed across the Channel, although at that moment in time such revolts seemed very distant from politics in British society.

The United States, race and Powell

Powell's attempts to resolve class differences were much influenced by these global reverberations of 1968. He attempted to craft an insular island politics that would protect the country from the dangers of the outside world. It was impossible, however, to ignore global events. In particular, America held what was already being described as a 'special relationship' with Britain, and events across the Atlantic were keenly reported on by the media. Images of the civil rights movement in the South and urban revolts in the North circulated widely in Britain.[43] The language of racism and anti-racism that was born out of American struggles strongly influenced the ways in which race was conceived of in Britain.

This transnational relationship was brought into sharp focus by Malcolm X's visit to the Black Country town of Smethwick in February 1965, nine days before he was assassinated in New York. Malcolm X had been planning a trip to Paris but he was unable to enter France and instead decided to fly to Britain, where he addressed the members of the Africa Society at the London School of Economics. The following day Malcolm X arrived in Smethwick, where Peter Griffiths had been elected as MP the year before. Malcolm X had been invited by the local Indian Workers' Association branch in the area, and members including one of the leaders, Avtar Singh Jouhl, provided a tour of the town. When asked why he had come to such a minor town, Malcolm X replied: 'I have heard that the blacks ... are being treated in the same way as the Negroes were treated in Alabama – like Hitler treated the Jews.' A BBC film crew had hoped to organise a meeting between Malcolm X and Griffiths, but Griffiths withdrew at short notice. Instead Malcolm X was filmed visiting Marshall Street, the street in which Griffiths had lent his support to a local council proposal to buy up property for occupancy by white residents only. Oppression such as that which was taking place in Smethwick, Malcolm X commented, would inevitably precipitate a 'bloody battle'. His advice to the local 'coloured' population was that they should not wait for Smethwick's fascists to construct gas ovens before they organise themselves.[44]

Unsurprisingly, Malcolm X's visit provoked outrage from the very racists he had powerfully attacked. The mayor of Smethwick stated that 'it makes my blood boil that Malcolm X should be allowed into this country. The whole news-getting side of the English world is endeavouring to turn Smethwick into Birmingham Alabama'. In the eyes of the mayor, Malcolm X's visit had constituted a breach of the peace.[45] A year later the visit and its filming continued to be a reference point for discussion. The *Observer* editorial commented that Malcolm X's interview with the BBC in the 'smouldering atmosphere of Smethwick' had been dangerous sensationalism, and should be remembered as television at its nastiest.[46] Malcolm X's presence was thus opposed by both liberals and conservatives, seeming to represent the dangerous possibility of future black resistance spreading from America to the West Midlands.

Powell's new fixation with immigration in Britain was framed by this bitter relationship with America. The part America had played in the downfall of the British Empire, and the British decision to become a junior partner in the American Empire, was something Powell would never forgive. In this sense, Powell argued that the very language of race was something that had been externally imposed on Britain by America. When asked about his belief in the inevitability of conflict, Powell argued that these were divisions based on political and social lines of nationality or even tribe, yet were not to be found within the biology of race. Instead Powell argued that race had come from the United States to 'distinguish Negro from non-Negro' but this was clearly a specialised and American acceptance of the term. The importation of American vocabulary into the circumstances in the United Kingdom, Powell argued, was 'dangerous and misleading'.[47] Powell's relationship with America ran deeper than distaste for the language of race. The animosity Powell held towards America flowed from his colonial past and he refused to forget that America had risen out of the Second World War while Britain had become a debtor nation incapable of maintaining 'imperial obligations'.[48] America had steamed ahead, exploiting the vacuum left by Britain's decline.

Powell visited America for the first time in November 1967. In July of that year Detroit had experienced one of the most deadly riots in American history with police shootings leaving forty-three people dead. The flames, blood and violence in the motor city would be seen across the world as a black working class were brutally repressed by the police. Powell's trip to America is described by a biographer as giving Powell's apocalyptical view of immigration its most profound boost, although of course those rioting were not migrants but black Americans.[49] Powell was apparently deeply disturbed at the racial tension that he found in American cities. He would for the following year receive regular newspaper clippings from a contact in Detroit on the unrest and racial violence going on there.[50] After his visit, Powell told an American journalist that 'integration of races of totally disparate origins and culture is one of the great myths of our time'. It had never worked throughout history, Powell argued, perhaps forgetting his rule about avoiding the language of race, and his comments of three years before on the positive impact of integration.[51]

Fresh from his return across the Atlantic, Powell made a sharp turn against immigration as the question of Asian immigrants from Kenya dominated political discussions. He soon found that there was a greater response to his comments on this than on any other of his subjects. On 19 November 1967 Powell addressed a packed meeting of Tories at Bournemouth, and when questioned afterwards about the continued growth in the immigrant population, he suggested that 'this is the American proportion' and stated the need for tougher control and voluntary repatriation. A few weeks later he spoke to his constituency association's general meeting of the folly which had already introduced into the country approximately one million immigrants from the Commonwealth and called for a drastic curtailment on the entry of dependents. He argued that no amount of misrepresentation would prevent the party and himself from voicing the dictates of 'commonsense and reason'.[52] Powell's new crusade in support of tighter immigration controls continued to be expressed in relation to his fixation with America. In December 1967 Powell protested vigorously to the BBC when the corporation showed an interview with the Black Power leader in America, Stokely Carmichael, in which Carmichael was asked by the interviewer, Patricia Philo, what he thought 'we Black people in Britain should do to liberate ourselves'. Powell claimed that the broadcast would 'have the effect of wounding and inflaming feelings'. The BBC apologised to Powell and agreed that showing the interview had been an 'error of judgement'.[53] Carmichael had already been banned from returning to Britain by the Labour Home Secretary Roy Jenkins, evidence of a broader panic spreading within British political circles on the potentially radicalising influence of the Black Power movement.[54]

On 4 April 1968, just sixteen days before Powell's 'Rivers of Blood' speech, Martin Luther King Jr. was assassinated in Memphis, Tennessee. King had travelled to Memphis to support African American city sanitation workers on strike against unequal wages and working conditions. In response to King's death, a series of riots spread across American cities as the non-violent road to civil rights seemed to have been brutally halted in its tracks. This violent spectre, and the movement of black resistance that flowed out it, was observed intently by Powell. Of course Powell was not interested in the violence of racism, but on the notion of a racial violence in which the oppressed is imagined as oppressor.

In the 'Rivers of Blood' speech, Powell talked of the 'tragic and intractable phenomenon which we watch with horror on the other side of the Atlantic'. He insisted that offering legal rights to so-called 'races' in Britain, through the Race Relations Act of 1968, would simply intensify the doomed route towards American society. Powell attempted to position himself as a prime interpreter of American dangers, to halt a process edging towards Britain. While racial tension was woven into the national fabric of the United States, it threatened to come upon the British Isles by 'our own volition and our own neglect'. In numerical terms, Powell warned, 'it will be of American proportions long before the end of the century'.[55] America, for Powell, had come to represent all that was wrong with how Britain conceived of immigration and the nation, serving as a lens in which to frame Powell's warnings of racial warfare in Britain.

The global anti-racist and industrial struggles of 1968 would translate into a British context over a longer period, with strikes and resistance coming to a head only in the early 1970s.[56] Yet the reverberations of

Paris, Detroit and Mexico City served as an immediate warning to British rulers. Powell's new politics of race was formed as an attempt at protecting England, or interchangeably Britain, from such global upheavals by forestalling them through a racially forged class compromise. The immigrant became the racialised symbol by which to illuminate this danger of instability and to stem the strikes beginning to take place within a multi-cultural workforce. While once an accepted part of the British economy, the place of Commonwealth immigrant workers had already been grad-ually encroached by successive governments. Powell both built on this legacy while carefully positioning himself as at odds with government policy, standing up for the little, local man against the pro-migration lib-eral establishment reigning in London. In order to visualise the immigrant threat in more meaningful ways, Powell was drawn to and relied on the respectable town of Wolverhampton as a place encapsulating his ideas of England.

2

The world in Wolverhampton

IN 1968, AS the world shook, Powell retreated to the provincial back-drop of Wolverhampton. The focus on this Black Country industrial town was entirely new to Powell's politics. He had never really been a constituency MP, and had spent little time in Wolverhampton, rarely seen in his constituency house by his neighbour, a Sikh bus driver.[1] Instead, Powell's permanent residence was in the highly desirable area of Belgravia in London and he spent only several weeks a year in his Wolverhampton residence.[2] Throughout the 1950s, Powell's political interest as MP had focused on Empire. His maiden speech in parliament, for example, was a passionate defence on the need for Britain to protect her colonies. Here, Powell called for the training of a new colonial army, and a redirection towards drawing 'far more than we do on the vast reserves of Colonial manpower which exist within the Empire'.[3] Powell could not have put it more clearly where his interests lay than in his election address of 1951 when he wrote: 'I BELIEVE IN THE BRITISH EMPIRE. Without the Empire, Britain would be like a head without a body.'[4]

The local issues of Wolverhampton were rarely, if ever, mentioned in parliament by Powell. Instead, Powell's politics focused on developing and promoting a new free market economic approach in Britain with Empire as its backdrop. However, as chapter 1 has demonstrated, the realities of decolonisation severed Powell's reliance on an imperial framework. This shift, in turn, created an urgent need for a new racial coding, both in terms of electoral gain but also ensuring that national stability prevailed. As racial ideologies of civilising missions and servitude began to unravel,

Powell offered a new enemy of the black immigrant at home. In this vein, immigrants who had once been welcomed to the country, by Powell himself, now became the enemy lurking within.

To make this threat visual, Powell mobilised a particular view of place, with Wolverhampton's past brought to life away from the global heights of Empire. There were descriptions of once 'respectable streets' and houses that were high in value because the property owners were decent, ordinary residents. Within this retelling, the people of Wolverhampton were historically white, reflecting the essence of a town that had been immune to change within a 'thousand years' of English history. Then the immigrants arrived. They bought the houses, terrorised the elderly women, and their children roamed the streets. The true residents remained white, but were fast becoming a minority within this occupied territory. These dramatic transformations in Wolverhampton provoked great fear to the extent that a 'For Sale' notice going up in a street 'struck terror into all its inhabitants'. Powell himself had experienced this terror, clarifying that he had lived within the 'proverbial stone's throw of a street which "went black"'.[5] In this way, Powell associated the landscape of Wolverhampton with racialised fantasies, both in terms of its naturalised whitened past and the deviation of a new black presence. A frozen history of Wolverhampton as stable, homogenous and white was contrasted with the chaos of the present, in which new 'invasions' from the outside were to be resisted.

Yet, as Massey argues, these new 'intrusions' were no more from outside, no more 'out of place', than many of the components of the currently accepted 'character of the place'.[6] This chapter examines the history of Wolverhampton and the ways in which it was constructed through social relations not only internal to it, but formed through a 'global construction of the local'.[7] Moreover, the presence of new migrants within the town was shaped by complex living and working arrangements that did not always correspond so neatly into the new racial categories Powell had highlighted. This chapter draws out these contradictions within Wolverhampton, examining the everyday experiences of residents within the town.[8] On the one hand, racism was interwoven into the lives of Commonwealth immigrants, determining the nature of work, leisure and living. Indeed, much of Wolverhampton was simply excluded to black immigrants. On the other hand, within the spaces that such immigrants were permitted, new forms of solidarity were also created, based not through race, but generated out of shared experience and exploitation, or common vulnerability. As Marx put it: 'In our days, everything seems pregnant with its contrary.'[9]

A brief history of the town

The history of Wolverhampton that Powell invoked gave the impression of a once stable and racially homogenous place. In reality, Wolverhampton was born out of and entangled in a global web of social relations, part of an imperialist chain which bound the lives of millions in the colonies to the urban town. Wolverhampton grew rapidly during the Industrial Revolution as a large town famous for its work making locks and iron goods of all kinds. In the nineteenth century a locomotive factory opened in the area and mines, furnaces and iron works all became central to the town and the wider Black Country.[10] These global chains of industry had produced great wealth and great suffering, both internally and externally. Most violently, the early history of industrialisation in Wolverhampton was integrated into the international slave trade in ways still uncomfortable to acknowledge within its public heritage.[11] The foundries and workshops of Wolverhampton produced chains, fetters, collars, padlocks and manacles, all of which would be taken to the ports of Liverpool and Bristol and used on the slave ships from Africa and in the British plantations during slavery in the Caribbean and North America. Such was the extent of this trade that Henry Waldram, a Wolverhampton ironmaker, advertised his specialism in the directory of 1770 as 'Negro Collar and Handcuff Maker'.[12]

This work was often based within smaller workplaces. Such conditions often led to a less organised and united workforce and pay was significantly lower than in other industrial centres of Britain in the nineteenth century. The closeness between employers and workers sometimes expressed itself in a form of civic pride which weakened class antagonisms. Nevertheless, resistance within these workplaces did emerge and in 1910 the women chain makers of Cradley Heath in the Black Country went on strike over their pitiful and unequal wages. There were national reports on the strike and the 'women slaves of the forge', demanding a salary which gave them the right to live.[13] The strike marked the start of the Great Unrest and the women strikers were finally victorious in the demands made to their own chainmasters.[14] The idea of a harmonious white race that Powell had propagated was therefore inaccurate.

Moreover, the working class of Wolverhampton had migrated from across the globe. During the era of slavery black people were shipped to Britain often in the capacity of personal slaves.[15] For example, in the eighteenth century there are records of George John Scipio Africanus in Wolverhampton. Mr Africanus was taken from Sierra Leone and given to the Wolverhampton Molineux family as a 'present' by a sea captain with connections to the Molineux family because of their financial involvement in Jamaican rum within the colonies. Mr Africanus was later apprenticed in Wolverhampton as a brass founder, a position that had been organised and allowed by his owners.[16]

While Powell talked then of an immutable white race, the reality within the town was more turbulent. Powell's family migration from Wales to the Black Country was not unusual as the workforce had always been drawn from elsewhere, a product of the avaricious employer demands for labour. Most significant within these waves of migration were the large numbers of Catholic workers who were attracted to the town from colonial Ireland, to such an extent that Wolverhampton had been known historically as 'Little Rome'. The greatest influx of this migration followed the Irish Potato Famine, when the mechanisms of colonial rule resulted in many young, single men migrating from Ireland in search of work in the iron works and mines of Wolverhampton and the Black Country. By 1871 the population of Wolverhampton had grown to 68,291 with an Irish population in excess of 12,000 so that nearly one in five of the population was Irish. Rather than simply an accepted section of the local working class, however, the Irish community often lived in the worst conditions of the area and were often portrayed as 'uncivilised'. Local police records document a monitoring policy by the newly formed police force in which the Irish were targeted as a criminal, suspicious grouping.[17] Powell's representation of an insular, homogenous people of Wolverhampton was therefore an illusion.

Expansion and new migration

During the Second World War, Wolverhampton became a key industrial site in the war effort when many of the engineering firms and factories were turned into the war ammunition sector. The war provided full employment and the mass expansion of working hours as many of the men within the town were enlisted to fight. Meanwhile those from the colonies played a vital role in providing Britain with much-needed military strength. Some of those soldiers from the Commonwealth were drafted near to Wolverhampton, where they were well received. After the war there was a popular feeling amongst workers across Britain of 'not going back' and people found a new confidence as they fought for the rights they had experienced in wartime to continue in times of peace. In the post-war period Wolverhampton experienced its own new industrial revolution. There was a huge expansion of industry and work flowed readily from this; the family businesses that had once provided the backbone of the local economy were falling to the multinationals. Small industries were rapidly being swallowed by large-scale firms, especially foundries and, in one case, a big tyre factory, Goodyear. As one journalist noted at the time, Wolverhampton was one of the places that had 'never had it so good', with very low unemployment and wage packets coming steadily from unusually stable industries.[18] Wolves FC won the FA Cup in both 1949 and 1960 and the victories seemed to represent the thriving nature of the industrial town in this period.[19]

Wolverhampton was therefore an attractive place for new migrants. In the first years after the war, migration to Wolverhampton was mainly white, from Italy and groups from Central and Eastern Europe. Many of these people already had connections with the town during the war; the Polish Brigade had been barracked nearby during the war, for example.[20] After the war there were around 12,000 'displaced persons' living in hotels in the Wolverhampton area. With huge numbers of employment vacancies to be filled, Wolverhampton became the first local authority to offer jobs to what were known as European volunteer workers.[21] On the local buses, for example, the Transport Department gave employment to fifty Poles, fourteen Dutch and six from elsewhere in Europe in 1949.[22] These groups had not always thought of themselves as white yet were able to racially dissolve, inter-generationally, into the local community. The story of Nicholas Ordinans, who grew up in Wolverhampton, gives a clear example of this process. Nicholas' father was a Polish Jew who had escaped from Germany via the Kindertransport in August 1939 at the age of fifteen. During the war he was first imprisoned in an alien internment camp and then assigned to farm work in the West Midlands, before going on to serve in Military Intelligence for the rest of the war because of his fluent German. At the end of the war he returned to the farm but decided to move to the nearest large town of Wolverhampton, where he secured a job at the nearby Goodyear Tyre Factory. He married a local and he insisted that his children were to have no involvement in the Polish community; he feared that they would face prejudice if they were known to be the children of a refugee. In fact Nicholas grew up having not been told anything of his father's foreign past, although he had his suspicions, and it was only as an adult that Nicholas would find out this history. Instead, Nicholas grew up perceiving himself as part of a white, Wolverhampton community.[23] Race was therefore a constantly changing phenomenon, in which the Jewish 'outsider' could, at a specific time and place, become part of a white Wolverhampton population.

This was not, however, the case for black immigration to the town. Before the war there had already been black people in Wolverhampton with records of a Jamaican working for the Baths Department in the 1930s. After the war these numbers increased, and many ex-servicemen, particularly from the Caribbean, began to drift back to Britain, drawn to industrial, urban centres with labour shortages. In June 1948 the *Express and Star* ran a story about seven ex-RAF Jamaicans who had emerged from a hostel for Polish refugees to look for work in Wolverhampton. 'We don't want to live permanently in a hostel' said one 'Ultimately we hope we can get lodgings with British families'.[24] Wolverhampton became a key town for such migration with thousands of people migrating from Commonwealth countries to find work and a new life.

Yet this experience of settlement in the town was quite different to their European counterparts, shaped as it was by colonial structures. For one thing, Commonwealth migrants often already had an in-depth knowledge of the 'motherland'. One Wolverhampton resident recalled growing up in St Thomas, Jamaica, where she attended school before migrating to Wolverhampton aged seventeen. In Jamaica they had 'learnt more about Britain at school than we did about Jamaica, so we knew quite a lot about Britain before we came here'. Meanwhile African history was not taught and the woman recalled that in school 'slavery was something to be ashamed of'.[25] Perhaps because of this colonial education, the idea of migrating to Britain was often met with great excitement and optimism. One Wolverhampton resident described his early childhood in a village in India, where he and the rest of his family worked in a field. The voyage to Britain as a young child was a dramatic contrast to this previous life, the man explaining: 'when you're in a village you don't know nothing about the outside world and when you see something like going in a ship, there's a film going on, on the top deck and free ice cream, free soda, free drinks and it's exciting, it's a new world you know it just opens up like a new world you know'.[26] Arriving in Wolverhampton, first impressions were often dominated by the smoke from the factories and the cold. In addition, many of those interviewed described the shock as a formal colonial knowledge of Britain clashed with the reality they now observed. One obvious difference was that the education those from the Commonwealth had undertaken was not reciprocal, as one man explains here:

> What I was surprised about is how the English people didn't know about us. And the teaching we had we knew about white people and as I say all of our legislation used to come from Britain and when you think about was what we'd been taught. Well, this England is the supreme to us and I felt OK we was backward according to that we was not in power and when I came here it was surprising to me

that people didn't know. Because it should have been known that
Britain had colonised all of these places and most of these places
the population was predominantly African Caribbean and from the
Asian background. So that was a surprise to me.[27]

In addition, on arrival to the town it became suddenly clear that white
people were not simply colonial masters but were also poor and working
class. A woman migrating from Barbados recalled in her first few days in
Wolverhampton:

> the greatest shock of all was when I saw white folks when I was
> going home in the car I saw white folks sweeping the street and
> white dustbin men. I said to my sister what's happening and she
> said they work the same as we do. Because in the West Indies you
> were taught to believe, because there was no television, there was
> no communication only what you read in *The Advocate*, the news-
> paper and what have you. We always put the white folks up on a
> pedestal we were taught to believe they were better than us.[28]

While colonial ideologies were unmasked in this way for Commonwealth
migrants, racial hierarchies could not be shaken off so easily. Unlike those
migrants with white skin, in this period those from the Caribbean and India
were marked out as different, and were unable to hide their migration histories from their children or the wider population. A man who worked as a
Methodist preacher in Wolverhampton recalled that growing up in Jamaica
they had viewed white people almost 'as god, we saw them as someone
perfect, very, very superior … I would like to have a white man's mind'.
Because of this upbringing, on arrival to Wolverhampton he had expected
that 'we would have been treated much better when we came here first. They
told us that we are subjects of this country and this is the mother country,
well I mean every child looks to mother'. Yet the reality was quite different:

> They called us you know to help them rebuild the country after
> the war, we sacrificed when we came here and we thought that we

would have had a good reception but we didn't get it that way, we had to beg and do everything to get a place to stop. There were places where you go and knock and they look at you, no room for you, they don't want no blacks and they don't want no Irish. Though I don't know why cos the Irish are white people so I don't know why. However, we, I didn't moan a lot, I stood my ground and said I'm going to stay put and I'm going to work hard and send down my roots and let the indigenous population know I have stamina in me.[29]

In the early years of migration, those from the Commonwealth struggled to find suitable housing in Wolverhampton and were forced to live in particular parts of the town. As late as September 1968 Wolverhampton housing committee regulations meant that 'immigrants' were forced to wait twice as long as everybody else before becoming eligible for a council house.[30] With severe shortages of council housing in Wolverhampton, many black people were therefore forced to rent, and in the first years many of those interviewed describing living four or five in one room with an outdoor toilet. For those who attempted to buy, it was considerably harder. Mr Balwant Singh, for example, was an Indian bus conductor in Wolverhampton who publicly demonstrated the discrimination he had experienced in housing. He had attempted to buy a house on a newly built private housing estate in Wednesfield for his wife and four children. When he inquired at an estate agent in Wolverhampton, however, he was told they had received instructions by the firm building the estate that they were not to sell houses on the estate to 'coloured people'.[31] For those houses that could be bought, a resident of Wolverhampton, Kirtan Singh, explained: 'A slum house in Wolves is not worth even £500. But we pay maybe £1200–£1300 plus for it. With this money the white family goes off and buys a new house in the suburbs. Those extra £700–£800 came out of our sweat.' Mr Dayabhai Patel continued: 'The only property we can buy is a slum house. Then the whites turn around and say we're creating slums.'[32] These problems of housing shortages, coupled with industrial change and the arrival of new workers, created the conditions in which

Powell could draw examples from his constituency. The forced concentration of immigrants in the deprived and decaying areas of Wolverhampton highlighted and reinforced existing social deprivation. Yet, as Sivanandan argued, it was racism which defined immigrants as the cause of these problems.[33]

Housing discrimination was often hidden from public view, yet in clubs and bars the exclusion of black immigrants was more visible. In 1955 it was acknowledged by a local journalist that a 'colour bar' existed in the town and 'we must face up to it'; 'Shall we encourage the formation of compact colour communities – little Harlems – in our midst?' the writer asked.[34] As new dance halls continued to open in the town, 'colour bars' became a common policy. Two separate 'West Indian dances' were organised, while the majority of dances completely excluded Commonwealth migrants, ensuring that white and black dancers did not mix. These divisions were not simply accepted, and the local paper wrote that 'dark-skinned immigrants who have brought their happy craving for music, singing and dancing from the Caribbean sunlight into the Black Country smog' were now demanding 'white girls at their dances'.[35] As a result, immigrant communities were keen to have a place of their own. Among the black people looking for a dance hall was Constantine Williams, who told the newspaper: 'We want to live like a piano: the black and white keys must play together. If we manage to get this place of our own we will welcome people of any colour, race or creed. There will be no discrimination.'[36] For the nine years before Powell's speech Williams and others had been seeking permission for such a venue, although they had been unsuccessful with the Town Hall, arguing such a licence would 'amount to segregation'. This was despite the fact that in Wolverhampton there already existed a Ukrainian club, two Italian clubs and a Hungarian club.[37]

In response to the racial segregation that existed, there was also serious resistance. The Scala ballroom in Wolverhampton became the most famous case operating a 'colour bar' in the town, with the management openly admitting that they followed such a policy. In 1958 they had refused to let Udit Kumar Das Gupta, a local Indian engineering draughstman, in to a dance. Gupta wrote to the mayor of Wolverhampton to complain and it was decided that the renewal of the Scala ballroom licence would have to be approved by the local magistrate, with their 'colour bar' policy in mind. By 1958 the Musicians Union was boycotting the ballroom and there were protests outside it. The local Labour Party opposed the renewal of the contract and the Labour MP John Baird took up the issue in parliament. Yet the magistrate decided finally to extend the licence of the Scala ballroom. Wolverhampton International Friendship League secretary Mr Murray Winmill stated despondently that that the 'colour bar has been officially upheld now and we can do nothing more'.[38] Despite this pessimism, the 'colour bar' was not popular and in a nationwide poll 62 per cent expressed their disapproval of the 'colour bar' at this Wolverhampton dance hall. Eventually the doors of the Scala were opened to all people when a new management took over in February 1959 and the 'colour bar' was lifted.[39] Meanwhile pub crawls were organised between the Indian Workers' Association and white students, exposing the 'colour bars' within the Black Country.[40] Segregation was therefore imposed on black communities within the town, and yet it was a policy that was increasingly opposed.[41]

Work in Wolverhampton

Despite this discrimination, Wolverhampton remained an attractive place for Commonwealth immigrants for the obvious reason that it was a town abundant with jobs. While in the early years following the war black migrants had often been prevented from employment, there were in fact not enough white migrants to fill increasing vacancies within Wolverhampton. This provided something of a conundrum, with the *Wolverhampton Chronicle* noting 'there are plenty of jobs and there are no people to fill them'.[42] At the time of writing in 1955 it was estimated that there were at least 1,200 vacancies in Wolverhampton. These vacancies were anxiously observed by employers, who recognised the confidence it had given to hired workers; 'if and when a man is dissatisfied with his job or if and when he becomes redundant, he can shop around for the type of job he wants to suit his capabilities'. An employment officer for a Wolverhampton firm summarised the situation thus: 'The supply of labour in the Midlands and in Wolverhampton in particular has not increased. The demand has been increasing constantly, yet there is not the slightest hope of the labour we require being supplied from local resources. What are we going to do?' The answer was given by another employment officer for a large foundry, who explained simply: 'Employ Jamaicans'. Six months previously this foundry had been desperately short of labour and although they knew there were Jamaicans looking for jobs the employment officer had been reluctant to hire them, anticipating 'labour difficulties'. But the situation had apparently become so desperate that his company would have had to restrict production if they had not hired more labour and he employed a few 'coloureds'. They worked hard and they were accepted by their fellow workers. This was a pattern reported on by a number of personnel officers of Wolverhampton large firms, with all acknowledging that the men were well received and favourably treated by their fellow workers.[43]

The routine experience of work, however, was framed by contradictory pulls. On the one hand, the large workplaces where Commonwealth immigrants were most likely to find employment brought those from different backgrounds together. The collective nature of work offered a more fluid, interactive picture that began to break down stark racial divisions between Commonwealth immigrants and white co-workers. On the other hand, these were still relations framed by racial stratifications inbuilt into the nature of this work. A sense of these dynamics was traced by the *Observer* when, in July 1968, national journalists from the paper were sent to explore Wolverhampton in the immediate aftermath of Powell's speech. It was observed that there were certainly sectors within the employment market of Wolverhampton where black immigrants struggled to find work. No 'coloured workers' could be found in the 1,000 members of staff in the large department store Beatties and neither were they present as clerks in the banks nor as sales assistants in public-facing jobs in Wolverhampton.[44] Another report highlighted that there was not one single 'coloured police officer' in the whole of the West Midlands police force.[45]

Instead, black immigrants of Wolverhampton worked mainly in transport, foundries, rubber moulding and other arduous factory jobs. Here, Roderick Ansine's story of finding work exemplified a common route into

Wolverhampton in this period. Mr Ansine had arrived in England after the hurricane of 1951 had wiped out his father's plantation in Jamaica. After six unhappy weeks in London he came to Wolverhampton. Although he had wanted to work as a mechanic, with no success he finally found work as a moulder in the town. He told the *Wolverhampton Chronicle*: 'I do not like the work very much, but I like the people. They have been swell to me – fair, you know, which is all we ask.'[46] Much of the work in the foundries of the Black Country was physically draining and could also be dangerous. There were many reports of deaths at work. For example, Mohammed Hassain had worked at a local factory for a year as a facing sand mill operator. Forty-eight years of age, he had moved to the Black Country to find work while his wife and family were still in Pakistan. In September 1968 Mohammed Hassain was killed working at an iron foundry when he was trapped in a facing sand mill. He was released by fellow workers, but was dead on arrival at the general hospital.[47] The tragedy was one of many reported on, and both immigrant and non-immigrant workers suffered from the hazards of such employment.

Workers were pulled together by the dangers of exploitation and yet race continued to mediate everyday experiences of work, with clearly defined limits to where and how black immigrant workers were tolerated. One local factory had 250 'coloured workers' out of a labour force of 1,300. The factory had eighteen shop stewards, of whom three were 'coloured', while there were thirty-five supervisors, all of whom were white. At a different factory a similar pattern was reported on, with 23 per cent of the workers 'coloured', two 'coloured' shop stewards out of a total of fifty, and 125 supervisors, all of whom were, yet again, white.[48] Of course, these racial hierarchies were neither accidental nor a natural outcome, but were actively promoted by employers. This was demonstrated when those same 'coloured workers' who had been hired, when officially attempting promotion were prevented from moving up the ranks. In one case a 'coloured' bus driver with fourteen years of service and, it was noted, a Wulfrunian accent, had applied for promotion to the role of inspector. He experienced no success although some white recruits trained by him had already been promoted above him. The management quietly ignored his application.

The trade union secretary told him frankly that 'white employees will not take orders from coloureds'. Similar examples of clear promotion block were reported on by 'coloured' nurses in the area.[49]

These hierarchies were informed and preserved through racial ideologies in which natural characteristics of submissiveness and superiority were imposed selectively on workers. The report on workplace relations in Wolverhampton highlighted that employers had hired 'coloured labour for its general servility and willingness to work long hours in poor working conditions'. Employers soon discovered, however, that their plans were not accepted with quite the servility they had expected. Indeed, it began to emerge that 'once the coloured workers are in a majority in a factory section, they can become quite militant, particularly if they have articulate coloured men in their ranks'. With some alarm, the report observed that in some cases 'coloured workers', particularly Indians, had either started unions where there were none, or had tried to make the old union hierarchy more responsive to their demands.[50]

Despite the militancy of these workers, racial divisions remained a serious hindrance to workers' rights in Wolverhampton in the 1960s. Race could become a category by which to perceive and relate to fellow workers in ways that strengthened the control of white employers. Sometimes this simply meant that resistance within the workplace was segregated and therefore weakened. The local paper reported on numerous spontaneous strike actions within workplaces in 1960s Wolverhampton that were often undertaken by separate racial groups with 'white workers' or 'colured workers' taking separate strike action, and sometimes even particular ethnicities such as Carribean or Asian workers. Often these strikes still had successful outcomes for the workers with employers agreeing to demands around break times and workplace conditions during a period when employment levels in the area remained high.

Yet in a number of cases racial division had serious implications for these disputes. In one factory in Wolverhampton a 'coloured worker' was asked to change his job and shift without any apparent reason except that he was a militant organiser. He refused to accept the order, was sacked, and in response all the 'coloured workers' came out in sympathy. Significantly, however, the white workers remained in work and not only that but they reportedly told the management to 'keep the wogs out' and that they were ready to work overtime to cope with production. The racism which existed within the workplace thus gave a green light to the management of the factory to assert their control. They then proceeded to sack 180 'coloured men'.[51]

There were a number of similar cases. At the Firth Vickers Stainless Steel factory in Blackheath, immigrant workers, mainly Asian, had been protesting that the company had been discriminatory in sacking more 'coloured workers' than white in a record redundancy. This was denied by the company and the men's union, the National Union of General and Municipal Workers, agreed that the redundancy had been fairly carried out. With the support of the union guaranteed and three days after Powell's speech on 23 April 1968, forty-four of these strikers were sacked for their protests against racial discrimination. Yet again the sacking of the forty-four strikers was not opposed by the union, who argued that their strike had been against union advice.[52]

Racial ideologies were therefore firmly rooted into the structure of the workplace. A memorandum from the Wolverhampton chamber of commerce to the Wolverhampton select committee stated that Asian and African-Caribbean workers seemed to be 'less able, particularly in the total time they have been in Wolverhampton, to accept the truly Western outlook on life, and they have certainly not been able to absorb the English way of life, which is so very different from their own'.[53] Propagating such racial divisions was evidently fruitful for employers.

Political responses and 'colour blind' love

Despite these divisions, in Wolverhampton neither Powell nor any other prominent politician showed opposition to the presence of Commonwealth immigrants in the 1950s and early 1960s. This was clearly demonstrated through the life story of Surjit Singh Sandhu. He was from a poor family but had studied a diploma in electrical engineering in India and when he passed his exams he decided he wanted to migrate to Britain to improve his life. His uncle was already living in Wolverhampton and Surjit was keen to join him. When Surjit went to the High Commission in India to get his visa he was refused entry into Britain. Surjit told his uncle who asked his local MP, Powell, for help and it was Powell himself who 'lobbied' the case. In response the High Commission gave Surjit permission to study in Britain and he migrated to Wolverhampton in 1965. 'I was so pleased, so when I arrived in Wolverhampton I went with my uncle to thank Enoch Powell. It was very nice actually he was quite a caring person to me you know? He said to me if you have any more problems you let me know.'[54] Powell explained to Surjit that he would help anyone who deserved support, as long as they had the correct paperwork. Surjit Singh Sandhu still has the letter from Powell lobbying on behalf of Surjit's visa request to Britain.[55]

The only sign of political opposition to migration in this period was the Birmingham Immigration Control Association in the early 1960s, a group pushing for restrictions to 'coloured people'. Yet it had little success, and its meeting in Wolverhampton, attempting to launch the group in the town, was met by opposition. The choice of location for the meeting was a direct provocation to the immigrant communities within the area, taking place in what the local newspaper described as 'Wolverhampton's Little Harlem'. While 'West Indians stood unconcernedly' in Waterloo Road, Staveley Road and Newhampton Road, Birmingham councillors and a leading employer were calling on the government to suspend immigration for a five-year 'breathing space'. Around 300 people crowded to listen to the speeches, yet amongst this number were a number of people attempting to break up the meeting. Soon after the meeting started, the secretary of the Wolverhampton Communist Party, along with Mr Stanton, a 'self styled champion of the coloured immigrants', began to protest. There were shouts of 'Keep fascism out of Wolverhampton' before such voices were ejected from the meeting.[56] The Immigration Association would not receive the support of Enoch Powell, and there is no found evidence of the group meeting again or progressing within the town.

Similarly, within the local papers in the 1950s there are very few, if any, letters of complaint towards Commonwealth immigrant settlement.

In 1956 the *Wolverhampton Chronicle* openly lamented the fact that it was 'unfortunate' that mention of problems surrounding the conditions of 'coloured workers' in Britain automatically suggested 'colour discrimination among people who have become hypersensitive since reading the harrowing accounts of Ku Klux Klan activities and negro-baiting from Tennessee'.[57] There was therefore recognition that there was not an appetite, locally, to discuss the 'problems' of 'coloured workers' in this period. Events in America loomed large in the town, just as they did nationally, and as the boom continued there was more evidence of curiosity and tentative forms of support developing between residents.

The reports on marriage illuminated such racial overlaps developing within the town. In 1952, a report focused on the marriage of two Jamaicans. It was noted that 'hundreds' had stopped to watch when the news got round that there was a Jamaican wedding on Queen Street, and 'curious gazes turned to murmurs of admiration' when Miss Joyce Richardson, the bride, employed as a nurse, stepped forth attired in 'dazzling white'. Inside the church well over 100 guests were waiting including many white friends of the couple. Their wedding was reported on with positive interest, with the headline that the pair from 'sunshine-land' were married in Wolverhampton.[58] Similarly, Rupert Allen's story gave an insight into a particular experience of Caribbean migration to Wolverhampton. He was interviewed in the *Wolverhampton Chronicle* in 1955, along with his wife Margaret, to tell readers of their interracial marriage. Mr Allen explained to the paper:

> Like many other Jamaicans I came to this country – during the war, to enlist in the fight against Nazism. We felt it was our fight, too, because we are brought up to regard ourselves as British – and you can imagine what we felt about Hitler's racial policy. I served in the RAF. I grew to love England and the people here. Everyone was so friendly, there was such a wonderful spirit of belonging together. When I went back to Jamaica and found that things were not good there – not much work, no prospects, I did not worry. I came back to England again. Maybe that was when I made my mistake. But if

I had not come back I should not have met Margaret – so it cannot have been a mistake. I came with six other lads from my home district in Jamaica.[59]

Mr Allen's story was laced with regret and painful experiences of racism, but they also coincided with his declarations of love for his white wife, Margaret Allen. They sat together with their two-year-old daughter, Pearl. Mr Allen added that love was 'colour blind', that love was 'heart calling to heart – the colour of your skin is unimportant'. Margaret Allen explained that her parents were against her marriage with Rupert but that they had 'gradually come round'. However, for Margaret it was still an ordeal sometimes to leave the house, with people staring at them and talking about how the 'coloured people' lived like 'filth'. Margaret wished that others would accept them and treat them normally, but added that the neighbours treated them with respect and were very kind.[60]

The experience of a 'colour blind marriage' was therefore filled with tensions but also acceptance by some within the town. Indeed many of the interactions reported on in the 1950s and early 1960s demonstrated that relationships were developing that complicated, if not challenged, racial divisions. An interview with a resident of Wolverhampton who had migrated from India illuminates some of these new forms of solidarity that were developing on an everyday level in the town. He had arrived in the town as a child in 1959 and described living in a street where 'our next door neighbour Mr Perry he was a real kind gentleman. He used to come around with a plate and say Mrs P can I have some curry please? And we used to go to him. All our neighbours and them who used to live in the next street they were all good'. In his secondary school when he first attended there were 'only about three Indian boys in our school and over five hundred white kids'. At school he used to watch his music teacher play the piano and he was 'fascinated' by the music. 'Then I hear Jimi Hendrix and I wanted to be like Jimi Hendrix playing a guitar you know so watching the teacher he says, one day he says you always watching me, would you like to learn about music?' From then onwards, the music teacher gave the boy guitar lessons after school and at fifteen he joined a band from school where they started 'going round the pubs'. They played

> English music because it was an English band, 5 of them white boys from my school and I was the only Asian in that group, right, so when they were talking about what we going to call ourselves, so the music teacher said he's a foreigner and the guy John he said why don't we call ourselves the foreigners. I said what do you mean foreigners, he said you're a bloody foreigner, so I said alright then … it was light hearted, oh we used to get called so many names [performing] but in reply to them, like Wog, they used to say you bloody Wog and I used to laugh it off because I say do you know what it means by Wog, well it means Western Oriental Gentleman. I am a Wog, OK, and that used to break the ice.[61]

Growing up in Wolverhampton in this period therefore created new forms of relationships, in which tensions were also tied together through friendships, both framed by and challenging of racial divisions. Such everyday relations were not unusual within the town. Yet by 1968 many of these tensions were beginning to increase. Racism had been a real force within the town, pushed by institutions and structures, but it had also been disorganised with no political leadership. It was an ideology often challenged through the varied and rich relationships formed between black and white people within the town, with the closeness of people necessarily creating new ways of living not determined by race.

With the end of the post-war boom, however, the centrality of racism became more real for an employer class keen to continue the control they exerted within the workplace. It was perhaps not surprising that many employers within the region were strongly opposed to the race relations bill proposed in parliament in 1968. In an article for the *Express and Star*, entitled 'Do we risk discrimination against whites?' the labour relations reporter argued there was a distinct fear among people closely connected with industry in the West Midlands that the bill would make immigrants a 'privileged minority in Britain', particularly in the field of employment.

A spokesman for the West Midlands Engineering Employers Association claimed that legislation was not needed for the problems of racial discrimination, arguing: 'I think it is highly probable that people will bend over backwards to show they are not being discriminatory, perhaps even to the extent of discrimination against white workers.'[62] Mr Fred Griffiths, the Wolverhampton district secretary of the Amalgamated Union of Engineering and Foundry Workers, agreed there was a danger that the bill would make people favour immigrants for fear of being accused of discrimination, even if there was no such intention. The article concluded that few people the reporter had spoken to could honestly say that they were not afraid that 'the experience of the US could be repeated here'.[63] Black immigrants did not, of course, become the 'privileged minority' that critics of the race relations bill had warned of after legislation was implemented. Even so, it was telling that employers, alongside Enoch Powell, prominently opposed anti-discriminatory legislation, while attempting to pitch white workers against black workers. This was not simply a trend within Wolverhampton but also reflected nationally, with the Confederation of British Industry partnering with the Trades Union Congress in first opposing the bill. The discussion and final implementation of the Race Relations Act in 1968 came at a time when Commonwealth immigrants within the workplace had initiated a series of small-scale strikes in opposition to this racial ordering. There was a strong fear within employer circles that racial divisions were beginning to unravel. Powell's speech then served as an intervention into this local scene, a way of deepening but also giving new direction to racial division within the town, as well as nationally.

3

Reverberations from 'Rivers of Blood'

O N 2 7 A P R I L 1968 a crowd of protestors marched through the streets of Wolverhampton, leaving St Peter's Gardens and bound for Dudley. They held homemade placards stating 'We back Powell and Britain', 'Freedom of Speech', while a large banner displayed the Union Jack with the capitalised ENOCH emblazoned on the middle of the flag. The image seen in figure 7 shows the demonstrators respectably dressed and there is a cheerful atmosphere as a woman eats her sandwich while marching past a row of houses.

Who were these people and why were they marching? It is hard to infer much from the photograph, except that all twelve of the figures that we can see, including the police officer, are white. Perhaps we can say that this was not an accidental fact when, at a specific place and time, Powell had imagined a white race separate from the interests and lives of the immigrant population in the area. For a short moment, Powell was successful in mobilising along these carved out racial lines. The previous chapter has demonstrated how the whole history of Wolverhampton was one of immigration, and that these movements necessarily created overlaps, interactions and moments of solidarity between those living in the area. Cutting against this, racism was inbuilt into the nature of work, housing and schools in significant ways. In the weeks and months that followed Powell's speech, however, it seemed as if the racial contours, which had already been present within Wolverhampton, were suddenly strengthened through their reformulation. 'He said what we were thinking' became the common local refrain reported on within the national press in response to Powell's words. Yet what had been thought of before Powell's outburst had been directionless. Powell provided a language and a defined form for those anxieties within Wolverhampton to coalesce. Within days of the speech, thousands of those very 'ordinary decent' people who Powell had invoked responded publicly to his speech. At a time of political and economic uncertainty, their actions illuminated the ways in which a specific section of the population came to think of themselves as white.[1] This chapter takes a closer look at how this reinvention of race played out in the immediate response to Powell's words. The speech was heard across the world as a 'racial explosion' in the centre of England, and these reverberations were proudly reported on by the Wolverhampton *Express and Star*.[2]

National responses

In the national news, the actions of the dockers in London attracted most attention, as a highly organised and powerful section of the British working class. Two days after the speech a thousand London dockers stopped work and marched to the House of Commons in support of Enoch Powell. Outside parliament they chanted 'We want Enoch Powell' while a protestor explained that Powell was 'the only man with the guts to say what he thinks'. Another group of dockers who had come out of an interview with Mr Powell exclaimed that talking to him had made them proud to feel British.[3] There were, however, individual voices of resistance within this. A spokesman for the Tilbury dockers told the *Times* that many dockers were 'disgusted' by the support shown to Powell.[4] While in a minority at this point, one London docker in the International Socialists, Terry Barrett, together with a small group of students attempted to dissuade the dockers from marching by distributing a leaflet which read:

> Who is Enoch Powell? He is a right wing Tory opportunist who will stop at nothing to help his party and his class. He is a director of the vast National Discount Company (assets £224m) which pays him a salary bigger than the £3,500 a year he gets as an MP. He lives

in fashionable Belgravia and writes Greek verse. What does he believe in? Higher unemployment. He has consistently advocated a national average of 3 percent unemployed. Cuts in the social services. He wants higher health charges, less council houses, charges for state education and lower unemployment pay. Mass sackings in the docks. Again and again he has argued that the docks are 'grossly overmanned'.[5]

The very presence of the leaflet marked the contested nature of Powellism in ways that would be important in future struggles in the docks. Yet in this case it was a failed effort. In London docks, twenty-five ships were idle and 4,402 dockers did not work during the action, according to the Port of London Authority.[6] The apparent contradictions of this action was often stressed within the national reports as dockers who had voted Labour all their lives now demonstrated support for a Conservative politician through political strike action. Amongst the celebratory scenes, however, there was real demoralisation within the London docks at the time of Powell's speech. The dock workers had lost a nine-week strike only a few months before the speech and had just accepted heavy redundancies.[7] All the men a journalist spoke to from the West India Dock were worried about the security of their jobs and their earnings.[8]

Meanwhile 300 meat porters from Smithfield market added to the protests in support of Powell. Wearing their white overalls and caps, there were speeches about English land and the spirit of Dunkirk, and chants of 'Enoch for Prime Minister!' Photographs show dramatic scenes of blood-splattered overalls on white men holding placards reading 'Smithfield says a George cross for Enoch'. The role of organised fascists in leading these walkouts was noted by reporters at the time, yet Powell had certainly tapped in to a feeling with a section of workers.[9] Across the country there were small token strikes with reports of walkouts of fifty engineering workers in Poplar, 100 tanker drivers at West Bromwich, and 350 gas plant construction workers at Ambergate, Derbyshire.[10] It was also evident that many of these strikes were treated in a very different way by employers. When fifteen workers at an agricultural machinery factory at

Huntingdon took strike action in support of Powell's speech, the managing director of MGB Engineering, Mr Karl Brooks, offered his support and explained to the press that his workers had taken action to show solidarity with Mr Powell but more than anything in support of free speech.[11]

In response to these scenes, the trade union leadership were noticeably quiet. The Trade Union Congress general council met soon after the speech yet decided they were 'keeping clear of the Powell question'.[12] At Scarborough, the president of the AEF, Mr Hugh Scanlon, said that in times of economic stress a scapegoat must arise, and today it was the coloured people. According to Scanlon 'exporting coloured people' would not solve the problems of housing, property, the aged or building hospitals.[13] Nevertheless the response from most trade unions was muted, with the transport union notably absent. Responding to the speech, Mr Jagmohan Joshi, general secretary of the Indian Workers' Association, believed the present trend of events in industry and employment showed that separate unions divided by race now had more chance of coming into existence in the near future and that this would be bad for the 'principle of trade unionism'.[14]

Of course, there was also opposition to Powell's speech. About 300 students from LSE marched to the house of Enoch Powell in Belgravia shouting 'Black and White, unite and fight' and 'Enoch Powell, we want you dead'.[15] A week after the speech a demonstration of 2,000 marched in protest at Powell, passing Downing Street and then to Powell's house 'in the heart of millionaire district of Belgravia', handing in several thousand letters calling on Mr Powell to withdraw his remarks. At Speakers' Corner, the Radical Students Alliance argued that logically Mr Powell should be calling for the Queen to be sent back to Germany and Prince Phillip to Greece. It was reported that during these speeches 'heated' arguments continually broke out, 'often between coloured and white people'.[16] Indeed in the weeks that followed the speech the unity of black and white people seemed ever more distant. The significance of this was sharply perceived by the minuscule and recently formed fascist organisation the National Front. They pointed out that their election prospects had grown enormously since the speech. 'Of course', said a spokesman, 'we had been saying for donkeys' years what Powell has at last belatedly come out with, but he has given it an air of respectability. We expect to do better in the elections as a result'.[17]

Meanwhile, new forms of black mobilisation were beginning to tentatively develop between different 'coloured immigrants' that Powell had identified in his speech. The immigrant enemy was not an all-encompassing term but a particular coded one used for those racialised immigrants from the Commonwealth. This process of identification created new forms of racial solidarity in which those very same immigrants began to self-identify and organise together, their 'pattern set on the loom of British racism', as Sivanandan put it.[18] The speech spurred Joshi and other black activists to host the first national conference of black immigrant associations in Britain a week later. Fifty delegates representing twenty militant immigrant organisations met in Leamington Spa to form the Black People's Alliance, discussing proposals to combat discrimination while pledging support for the 'unity of coloured people' in Britain. Joshi, the new convenor of the Black People's Alliance, explained: 'We have decided to go all out to consolidate and strengthen the relationship between black people in this country coming from different origins.' Asked if there was any suggestion of violence, he replied: 'We are not the people who create Detroits, Detroits are forced on us.' Mr Powell's speech had simply 'hardened' their attitude to racial discrimination while bringing them closer together.[19] Blackness then became a way of resisting Powell's racial impositions, drawing guidance and inspiration from the politics of Black Power in the United States. The Black People's Alliance went on to organise a demonstration of 4,000 people a few months later outside Rhodesia House, where thousands called for an end to racial discrimination. The *Sun* reported that the 'stunning thing about the march was not the shrill shouts and caterwauls of the seasoned marchers. It was the stony, impassive faces of the Indians and Pakistanis who had travelled from towns like Wolverhampton, Nottingham and Leamington Spa to protest about racial discrimination'.[20] An effigy of Enoch Powell taken from a coffin was set alight with chants of 'Disembowell [sic] Enoch Powell' (see figure 3).[21]

Local support

These national responses were magnified in the industrial town of Wolverhampton, albeit with their own local inflections. Following the speech, Wolverhampton was branded as 'another stage' in the progression from Notting Hill to Smethwick and the impact of the speech was experienced with a sharper intensity in the area.[22] The words of the speech were translated into the area in varied ways. In mixing the classical ancient poetry of Virgil's *Aeneid* with new fantasies of racial warfare, Powell's metaphor offered scholastic legitimacy to a new way of thinking, a way of publicly saying what previously could not have been said and had only been tentatively imagined. When a national journalist visited Wolverhampton three months after the speech and asked white schoolchildren what they thought of Powell's words, one responded: 'The blood will flow – that's what he said.' Another schoolboy added 'That's right, he only went the long way round saying send the lot back home'.[23]

This interpretation of the speech led to polarised responses within Wolverhampton. In the weeks following the speech there were, in the words of the local paper, a 'rash' of protests, counter protests, strikes, petitions and mass votes in response to the words of Powell. Wolverhampton was pushed into the limelight and a number of white workers publicly declared their pride in 'our Enoch' to the wide range of national journalists now sent to the town with a newfound interest in their views. This support also expressed itself in strike action. Two days after the speech fifty steel erectors employed at Rugeley B power station took part in a token strike in protest at Powell's dismissal from the shadow cabinet. A representative of the Rugeley strikers commented: 'We feel the sacking of Powell was undemocratic. We do not necessarily agree with his views but we do support his right to express them.' Their employers clarified that 'there is no industrial dispute between these men and the company. They have told us they are simply voicing their protest in the best way they know at the sacking of Mr Powell'.[24] Meanwhile it was reported that roughly a thousand men from Norton Villiers, the Wolverhampton engine manufacturer, finished work half an hour early to make a gesture of support for

Powell. They agreed to work later the next day so that production would not suffer.[25] Other workplace petitions in support of Powell's speech were reported on, with one thousand of the 1,200 employees at Joseph Sankey, GKN Works in Bradley, Bilston signing a petition.[26]

Much of this action in Wolverhampton appeared to be uneven and often sporadic. One of the men from Bayliss Jones and Bayliss, a Wolverhampton firm which manufactured nuts, bolts, iron fencing and spikes, described their action in support of Powell as 'a spontaneous move on our part. We heard what the brewery workers were doing and we decided to join them because we believe they are right in supporting Mr Powell's right to free speech'.[27] Three days after the speech a protest took place in Wolverhampton to show further support for Powell, on the day of a parliamentary debate on the Race Relations Bill. Brewery workers led the march surrounded by homemade placards, with slogans such as: 'Enoch: the man that cares about us'. The placards illustrated that many of the protestors had joined the march from their workplace, with a man and a woman holding up another cardboard sign simply stating: 'HP SAUCE SUPPORTS ENOCH POWELL'. Cheers were made as a branch official of the Transport and General Workers' Union posted a 250-signature petition to Heath.[28] The protest was no bigger than a few hundred at most, however.

Indeed, there were tensions within this workplace support. Many trade unions actively discouraged their members from joining the action and some local trade union councils in the West Midlands put out statements against Powell's speech. The Warley Trades Council, for example, commented that those who most visibly showed their support for Powell were the least active within the union movement; 'that men should come out on strike for a thing like this is disgusting' concluded Mr Charles Johnson, from Old Hill AEU union branch.[29] Mick Powis was, at the time, a trade union shop steward in a large engineering company called Turner Manufacturing based in Wolverhampton. He recalls:

On the shop floor after the weekend it was the main topic of conversation for several days. It has to be said there was widespread support for Powell. Probably summed up by this quote 'Enoch Powell is a fine gentleman, who is saying what everybody thinks'. I was subject to a lot of banter of the 'good old Enoch' variety as people knew my political views. There was talk of a token strike to support Powell. This led to a shop stewards meeting which was one of the few which ended with a unanimous decision not to support it. The left argued that Powell was a racist; and from the right that they wouldn't support political strikes. As far as I remember there was no violence or threats to individual black workers, though there was some pro Powell banter.[30]

The response of workers was therefore debated seriously in the days following the speech, and where there were organised trade unionists they were often able to prevent large-scale strikes in support of Powell. In contrast, the employers within the area were remarkably indulgent to the walkouts. A partnership between workers and employers was often demonstrated in support of Powell, with the brewery men who remained in work stating they had done so 'to avoid hurting the company' and agreeing to donate their afternoon's pay to charity or to Powell's political fund.[31] At a number of the workers' walkouts reported on by the local newspaper, the directors of the firms also walked out in solidarity with Powell and 'free speech'. In a more official, formal setting, the Wolverhampton Chamber of Commerce met to discuss the speech and provided qualified agreement to Powell's speech, a spokesman stating: 'Insofar as Mr Powell stated facts, we must obviously agree with him.'[32]

This cross-class collaboration was reported on by the local paper as a sort of community celebration in the town, with pages of reports in the days following the speech filled up with examples of community support for their MP. '"Back not sack" is local cry', was the paper's front-page headline four days after the speech.[33] Two weeks after the speech, the paper stated that the response to Powell had surely been one of 'the most incredible fortnights in the country's history'.[34] On one protest in support of Powell it was reported that the workers, perhaps ironically, adopted the hymn of the civil rights movement, 'We shall not be moved', as their anthem, also accompanied by the singing of 'We have the best MP in the land'. At another demonstration a few days later, marching from Wolverhampton to Dudley, protestors met outside a meeting where Heath was speaking on his first visit to the West Midlands after the speech. The songs were less nuanced here, with the words 'Send them back to Pakistan. Hallelujah' repeatedly sung.[35]

Coordinated exclusions

Within these reports, black immigrants were noticeably absent from such 'local support'. They appeared occasionally as unexpected, unwanted figures within this activity, occupying a sinister space within the excitement of the town. At the Victoria Sheet Metal Company in Wolverhampton, the petition in support of Powell was signed by sixty-one workers, drawn up on the initiative of men on the shop floor. The newspaper ominously noted that the firm did have one immigrant, an Indian, amongst the workers. This isolated, anomalous figure was swiftly forgotten and instead the article concluded with a statement from the spokesperson of the petition that 'It has not been made out of any racialist feeling but in a sincere belief that Enoch Powell has at least been honest and is trying to face up to a genuine problem'.[36]

Similarly, at the Dudley protest in support of Powell, it was noted by the paper: 'There were hardly any coloured people to be seen in the area, but two – one of them wearing a bus conductor's uniform – had to run a gauntlet of boos and hisses as they left the town hall.' As we will see in the next chapter, the bus workers were still involved in an ongoing struggle for the right to wear the turban. Suddenly one of their ranks found themselves amongst a protest in support of Powell. The bus conductor, at this moment, was outnumbered. For the *Express and Star*, the nameless presence of such racialised people were represented as obstructive forces, outside of the true constituency that the newspaper was concerned to report on in the heat of the 'Rivers of Blood' moment.[37]

Of course, the actions in support of Powell did impact on these silenced figures, controlling the spaces that racialised immigrants were and were not permitted to enter. The previous chapter has discussed a range of 'colour bars' which stopped black people from entering spaces in Wolverhampton. Sometimes these were unofficial, and often these were simply rules that had been little discussed publicly, what Sivanandan describes as the 'laissez faire' of racism in the post-war period.[38] But in the days following the speech, the 'colour bar' in Wolverhampton would become an explicit way of demonstrating support for Powell's words. The North Wolverhampton Working Men's Club was located in an area where many black immigrants lived. It had for ten years followed a 'colour bar', yet this had recently been challenged following a complaint by a black woman, Miss Ruth Saxon. Saxon had been turned away from the club after she attempted to enter with her friend, who had been invited to perform for the club as a 'strong man'.[39] Due to the complaint of Saxon and her friend, a vote within the club was planned to decide if the 'colour bar' would be continued yet, coincidently, this vote took place a day after Powell's 'Rivers of Blood' speech. A unanimous vote of 800 people voted to keep the club doors shut to 'colour' (see figure 6). 'No person with dark skin will be admitted to the premises' they stated, whether or not he or she was a booked artist, guest or affiliated member. The only abstention came on the second vote, from Mr Frank Smith, the previous year's Labour mayor of Wolverhampton, who argued that without a discussion on the matter he could not vote in its support. To the local newspaper Mr Smith clarified that the ban on 'coloured' people as members was the correct decision, adding 'I would at the present time agree that our coloured friends need a little educating in our ways'.[40] The secretary of the club since 1955, Mr George Hall, explained to the *Observer* that 'we've the right to keep them out ... Our members live by them and they know what it's like. All this dirt and sex. There are areas in this town where a white woman wouldn't dare walk down the street. If they'd come in small numbers like the Italians there wouldn't have been a problem. But they breed like rabbits'.[41]

In part Mr Hall's racism stemmed from a colonial racism that he acknowledged, explaining: 'my generation was always taught that black was dirty and white was clean. We were taught about the Black Hole of Calcutta, the Zulu War and all these atrocities perpetrated by the coloured people'. He concluded 'That was what our education was about, and now, when the country's being flooded with coloureds, we've got to go and revise our ideas'.[42] Mr Hall had clearly held deeply racist perspectives for some time, and yet his confidence to articulate these thoughts was strengthened by Powell's words. Indeed, the vote to continue the 'colour bar' had taken place at an opportune time for the club secretary, and he had managed to secure support from 800 white residents of Wolverhampton. The vote was also defended by the current mayor of Wolverhampton, Alderman Robert Campbell, who felt strongly about the rights of the club to block non-white members: 'A club is a club. The idea is for people of a similar outlook to meet'. In response to this vote, both the Musicians' Union and British Equity announced in a statement they had instructed members not to accept engagements at the Working Men's Club, and there were also local reports of 'Black Muslim' organisations threatening to burn down the club and of death threats to the owner.[43]

Within this climate, the weeks following the speech were dangerous times for racialised minorities in Wolverhampton. In the fortnight following the speech, twelve separate incidents of racist violence in Wolverhampton were recounted to a national reporter.[44] One attack reported on ten days after the speech was a 'slashing incident' involving fourteen white youths chanting 'Powell' at a black christening, although the two godparents present were both white. Despite their presence, 'one West Indian, Mr Wade Crooks', a moulder and resident of Wolverhampton, had to have eight stitches over his left eye after being cut with a 'flashing object'. His son, Mr Albert Crooks, whose child was being christened, was treated at an eye infirmary after being punched. Mr Wade Crooks, with a plaster over his eye, told the paper:

> After the christening one of the white men suggested that we should go into a pub, the Dan O'Connell, on the East Park estate. When we came out I saw a group of white chaps by the door. I heard my son shout that he had been hit. We went towards the car and the crowd were shouting 'Powell, Powell' and 'Why don't you go back to your own country?' Someone punched me as I sat in the

car, I was hit across the eye. When I sat down somebody pulled something from his top left hand pocket. It flashed across my face. I pulled my head back as it came again, and it flashed across and touched my lip. I have been here since 1955 and nothing like this has happened before. I am shattered. One thing I don't want is reprisals, but I fear there will be trouble if I don't get justice.[45]

Mr Wade Crooks added: 'We had to report this to the police three times before they came. Our experience is that if they hear a coloured man's voice on the telephone they won't come and they don't want to know.'[46] The impact of the speech was felt so intensely that members of the West Midlands Caribbean Association formed a new measurement in time to mark the recent wave of racist attacks; BE and AE, 'Before Enoch' and 'After Enoch'.[47] Moreover, the lack of police support meant self-defence became a vital necessity within the area. Mr James Woodward, a Wolverhampton Labour councillor, had already noted this reality immediately following the attack on the Crooks family, commenting: 'I have known Mr Crooks since 1955. He is a good man. If coloured people feel there is no protection for them in this town they will organise themselves into protection bodies.'[48] Members of the Indian Workers' Association in the area recalled the dangers of walking home alone, and did indeed organise defence groups to protect Indian migrants from racist violence.[49] Avtar Jouhl of the Birmingham Indian Workers' Association recalled that the committees were immediately set up to organise this protection; 'we will not sit back, we will hit back' the organisation announced.[50]

Yet in the weeks following the speech there was a real fear that pervaded immigrant communities targeted by Powell's speech. Anand's father was a migrant from India who had worked in a Wolverhampton foundry and remembered the strong impact of the speech; he 'lived in his suitcase', always ready to leave the country, telling his children that 'one day they might be sending us back'.[51] This impact was powerfully described by Mrs Jan, who had moved from India to Wolverhampton with her husband in the late 1950s. Her husband found work quickly in the Sankey foundry of the town, although he was a qualified teacher in India;

'that's what all the Indians were doing here' Mrs Jan explained. When Mrs Jan arrived in Wolverhampton she explained 'it was such a shock because when we were living in India we thought England was a place like heaven on earth or something'. They lived in a terraced house they had brought together with a friend from India 'because at that time ten or twelve people used to all of us live in the same house'. Soon after Mr Jan lost his job in the foundry, 'at that time in the industry they were hiring and firing like anything', and people could easily find work elsewhere 'you could change your job three times within a week, because there were so many jobs'. Mr Jan decided instead to find work in the schools and became the first Asian schoolteacher in Wolverhampton, working in Whitmore secondary to help teach children English who had recently arrived from India. By that time more of their friend's family had arrived from India to live in the house and the Jan family decided they needed a place of their own and they found a semi-detached house to buy with central heating and a nice garden in Segley. They put in the bid and the owners accepted their offer of £3,000. Mrs Jan explained:

We were very pleased that we found a house. But it was the night before Enoch spoke. And when he spoke we heard his speech we were scared. We thought now we'll have to leave the country. And so my husband he went and he said to the lady, we didn't have a telephone at that time, he told the lady I'm sorry we'll have to pull out, we can't manage it. So we pulled out and we didn't buy that house because we were so scared. Because Enoch, and actually all of the Conservatives, they were the same actually, they were all saying we couldn't be here anymore, we were a burden here, when actually we were contributing to the economy, all the jobs English people didn't want to do Asian people did or West Indian people did. The country needed so many people to build up the country. So yes we didn't buy the house. And then we were still thinking oh the children are growing up they will need their own bedroom. But it took us another five years to feel secure to put a deposit on a different house.[52]

Local opposition

Within this climate of fear, in the months following the speech the response from immigrants in the town was at first defensive. In the early days this emerging movement sought inspiration from across the globe and particularly the civil rights movement in America. Two days after the speech, two memorial services took place for Martin Luther King in different parts of Wolverhampton. At the parish church it was reported that 'a large congregation of white and coloured people' ranging from the mayor to Catholic dignitaries paid their tribute to racial equality.[53] These services had been planned before Powell's outburst, and hundreds attended, serving as perhaps the first meeting point for anti-racists within the town to take stock of the new situation, while demonstrating their grief that King had been assassinated.

'Wolverhampton knows how to deal with its racialists' the secretary of the Wolverhampton Communist Party, George Barnsby, proudly declared a week after the speech. 'The people of Wolverhampton know Enoch Powell' Barnsby continued, 'he has peddled his Stone Age anti-working class views on every subject under the sun in this town for 18 years. The man yearns to be Prime Minister and thinks he can achieve his aim by winning support from the most prejudiced sections of the population'.[54] In truth though there was uncertainty amongst the left within the town in how to proceed and anti-racist responses were disorganised. The slogan of the local Communist Party printed on thousands of leaflets following the speech was to 'Keep Wolverhampton Civilised!'.[55] This highly ambiguous slogan reflected confusion and uncertainty within the ranks of the labour movement in how to respond to questions of immigration that Powell had unleashed. There were two other MPs representing Wolverhampton, both Labour, who spoke out against the speech. Renee Short, the MP for North East Wolverhampton, launched a 'bitter attack on Powell and co.', lamenting 'whoever heard of anything like the dockers marching to support Enoch Powell. He is against everything they have ever fought for. He is against trade unions and the working class'.[56] Similarly, Mr Bob Edwards, general secretary of the Chemical Workers Union and MP for

Bilston, argued that it was 'absolutely disgraceful that trade unionists should be dragooned into this race campaign. It is dead against the spirit of international brotherhood on which the trade union movement was founded. It is a retrograde step for any trade unionist to stop work on an issue like this when they have to work with immigrants in industry'.[57]

In addition, many of the immigrants who Powell had targeted within the speech became compelled to organise against the backlash. In 1954 the Wolverhampton Council for Racial Harmony had been formed with a range of different parties in support and with full-time offices and workers.[58] The secretary and liaison officer for the group, Mr Aaron Haynes, told the *Wolverhampton Chronicle* that the speech by Powell was a deliberate attempt to sink the Race Bill. In spite of the speech, which in Mr Hayne's estimation was both 'provocative' and 'insulting', there was still a possibility that racial co-existence could be realised. But he concluded that the road was now more difficult.[59] Similarly, there was a sharp reaction to the speech from the West Midlands Caribbean Association, with an emergency meeting called and the MP described as the 'notorious Titus Oates' inciting racism. Mr Joe Hughes from the group explained that 'unlike our brothers in America who are still fighting for the vote we have got it, but it is no advantage' with no representation for the 'coloured community' in parliament. The group began a petition protesting Mr Powell's comments which was to be sent to the prime minister. Much to their anger, Powell refused to meet with the association, while on Saturday night he had been seen 'laughing and drinking with immigrants' at the Italian Community Association's dance at the Wulfrun Hall. 'Why could he not similarly recognise other coloured people?' Mr Hughes asked. Yet the association continued to urge restraint; it was important to fight, one member stated, but not with the sword.[60]

In partnership with these groups, the resistance was in the first few weeks organised by local students, coinciding as it did with a high point of unrest within the colleges and universities of 1968. Students from the College of Art and Technology in the town began to organise a protest on the very day when Powell returned to Wolverhampton, or as the students put it, the day the 'jackal returned to his den'. More than 300 protestors marched through the town, calling for 'racial harmony' and launching an appeal for volunteers to give a couple of hours a week to help the work of the Wolverhampton Council of Racial Harmony.[61] These protests were led by students and would continue to follow Powell, with a number of speaking occasions having to be cancelled because of student protests. In December, for example, Powell was forced to walk out of a meeting at the Wolverhampton College of Art and Technology after constant interruptions and uproar.[62] A year later, the town would again be returned to, now for a national demonstration marking Powell's speech and the racism that had been unleashed. Over a thousand protestors marched in the heart of Powell's constituency as part of the black and white unity campaign in the area organised by a new coalition between the Indian Workers' Association and left-wing organisations. Protestors explained that Enoch Powell had made the situation of immigrants in the town a national issue and that their protest served as a counter-offensive to what was becoming an 'apartheid town'.[63]

These were some of the first, explicit responses to Powell's speech. A small section of white workers, in support of Powell, took political strike action, and while this action seemed larger and seized the headlines, students and immigrant groups were also beginning to organise resistance to the speech. In Wolverhampton, many of the larger workplaces were now multiracial in form. Taking action in support of Powell meant, implicitly, challenging colleagues within the same workplace. This did occur as the story of the petition signed at Victoria Sheet Metal Company in Wolverhampton makes clear. For the lone Indian immigrant worker within the company, the petition was a way of clarifying that he was not accepted within the workplace. Such divisions suited local employers within the town, and they often encouraged such action in support of Powell. Yet for the vast majority of workers and trade unionists in Wolverhampton, as elsewhere, there was a quieter listening to Powell's speech taking place. There was, rather than overwhelming support for Powell within the workplace, muted confusion. For example, the workers within the two largest factories in the town, Goodyear and Courtaulds, did not respond publicly either way to Powell's words. The labour movement were also disorientated, mainly refusing to comment, and while some unions offered oppositional statements to the speech, this did not provide a direction for how to challenge the racism taking hold within sections of the country. Beneath the surface, however, new forms of resistance were taking place in Wolverhampton, actions and ways of living that challenged Powell's words not yet in a direct form, but instead taking place on an everyday level.

Opposition to Powell's race warnings overflowed on to the streets in the late 1960's

Figure 1 Protest against Enoch Powell in Wolverhampton, late 1960s. Express & Star Newspaper Ltd.

Wolverhampton workers
from a brewery and factories
march through Wolver-
hampton today in support
of Mr. Enoch Powell. The
walk ended at the town hall
when a letter was posted to
Mr. Edward Heath by Mr.
Kevin Denny (above).

Figure 2 Protest in Wolverhampton, reported on 24 April 1968. Express & Star
Newspaper Ltd.

Figure 3 Protest called by the Black People's Alliance outside Rhodesia House, reported on 12 January 1969. Express & Star Newspaper Ltd.

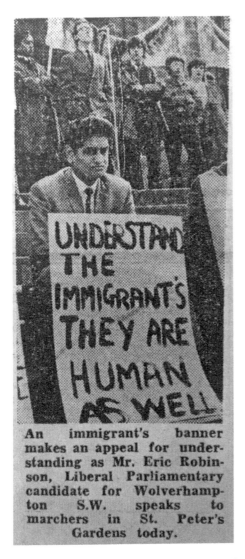

An immigrant's banner makes an appeal for understanding as Mr. Eric Robinson, Liberal Parliamentary candidate for Wolverhampton S.W. speaks to marchers in St. Peter's Gardens today.

Figure 4 Protest in Wolverhampton, reported on 4 May 1968. Express & Star Newspaper Ltd.

Figure 5 Protest in Wolverhampton, reported on 24 April 1968. Express & Star Newspaper Ltd.

Figure 6 Vote in North Wolverhampton Working Men's Club, 22 April 1968. Express & Star Newspaper Ltd.

Figure 7 'Marchers supporting Mr Enoch Powell on the Dudley Road today after leaving St Peter's gardens bound for Dudley', reported on 27 April 1968. Express & Star Newspaper Ltd.

Figure 8 Mike and Ray in West Park primary school, a photograph disseminated by the *Sunday Jamaica Gleaner* in the 21 April 1968 issue. ZUMA Press, Inc. / Alamy Stock Photo.

4

Resistance in the schools and on the buses

Powell's new racial politics focused on the 'privileges' that immigrants in Wolverhampton were allegedly receiving. White constituents, in turn, became the victims. The 'existing population', according to Powell, found 'their wives unable to obtain hospital beds in childbirth, their children unable to obtain school places, their homes and neighbourhoods changed beyond recognition; at work they found that employers hesitated to apply to the immigrant workers the standards of discipline and competence required of the native-born worker'.[1] Powell's speech served as an intervention into an unsettled racial landscape of Wolverhampton that was by no means accepted. Indeed, in targeting the figure of the immigrant, those same racialised subjects began to contest such impositions. The previous chapter discussed the explicit responses to Powell's words. Yet there were also latent tensions simmering within Wolverhampton, sometimes messy, unclear and everyday struggles as Commonwealth migrants began to collectively assert their rights. These actions were registered by Powell who, during the run up to his 'Rivers of Blood' speech, wrote to Heath: 'I find in my constituency in the last few weeks an ominous deterioration, which is taking the form not of discrimination by white against coloured but of insolence by coloured towards white and corresponding fearfulness on the part of white.'[2] This chapter explores in detail the resistance, or what Powell described as the 'insolence', of such immigrants in the town. The chapter first examines these dynamics within the workplace, with a particular focus on a dispute on the local buses. The chapter then moves on to the school setting and the ways in which immigration was framed in the town's schools. Both the schools and the buses had become critical examples within Powell's new racial politics. Yet what was happening on the ground seemed to suggest new ways of living and working that challenged fixed racial boundaries.

The turban dispute

The turban dispute on Wolverhampton buses between 1967 and 1969 was a prominent example of workers organising to challenge racial impositions from above. Powell himself in both his 'Rivers of Blood' speech and his Walsall speech referred to the turban dispute and described the actions of the Sikh workers as an example of dangerous and lurking 'communalism'. This political framing attempted to separate the Sikh bus workers from the 'local' working class by claiming that the Sikh bus workers had cultural needs that clashed with the host country. Media reports similarly removed the turban dispute from the dynamics of the workplace and class relations. The BBC, reporting on the dispute in the town, commented that 'Back in 1921 the people who ran the Transport Committee then laid down that drivers and conductors should wear the uniform provided, and nothing but the uniform provided. They hadn't thought then of turbans coming into their town except perhaps when Ali Baba was the Christmas pantomime'.[3] The dispute on the buses was represented as an intriguing curiosity with exotic cultures attempting to change age-old British rules. To different degrees, the small academic literature on the dispute has mostly perpetuated this analysis, situating the struggle as that of a cultural clash with the turban understood simply a signifier of religious difference.[4] Instead, the dispute must be contextualised within the labour movement and a longer history on the buses of racism, class and resistance. The demand to wear the turban was part of a struggle in which immigrant workers demanded recognition as a legitimate section of the organised working class.

Wolverhampton's buses experienced serious staff shortages in the post-war period. The low wages and bad working conditions of the job meant that employers had historically hired immigrants from a range of backgrounds. This was pointed out years later by a spokesperson for the Wolverhampton Trades Council who was asked in a select committee on race relations whether the proportion of 'coloured busmen' now stood at about 75 per cent 'immigrants'? The trade unionists responded: 'You say immigrants. On the buses our first influx of immigrants consisted of displaced persons after the war. Many of them have grown up with the jobs and some are now retiring. When you refer to "immigrants" I take it you mean our coloured brothers and sisters.'[5] The focus of the committee, with the coded language aimed at categorising migrants by skin colour, reflected the spread of a wider political trend targeting Commonwealth immigrants that Powellism had intensified.

The buses, then, became a heated site where these racial divisions played out. In 1955 this erupted when a union dispute was initiated over the new hiring of 'coloured' workers on the buses in West Bromwich. Strike action and pickets were organised every Saturday in protest at the employment of an Indian man, Mr Patel, as a trainee conductor.[6] Mr Prem, an Indian immigrant activist, wrote to the Indian High Commissioner in London over the strike, arguing 'The West Bromwich strike is in the nature of a test cast. If the strikers succeed in getting this man dismissed, the way will be open for other similar dismissals'.[7] Inspired by the action of workers in West Bromwich, a few months later the bus workers in Wolverhampton also took strike action, demanding a 5 per cent limit on 'coloured immigrants' employed on the buses. At that time there were sixty-eight 'coloured workers' employed on the buses amongst a total of just over 900 in Wolverhampton. The branch secretary of the union, John Cooney, explained that they had originally been prepared to accept a figure of fifty-two 'coloured workers'. He told the press: 'We are not operating a colour bar. The men have made friends with the coloured men on the job, but we don't intend to have the platform staff made up to its full strength by coloured people only.'[8] The Labour MP for North East Wolverhampton prominently opposed the strike action and issued a statement demanding the Transport and General Workers' Union (TGWU) clarify its position on the 'colour bar issue'.[9] The secretary of the bus workers' union responded that their action was 'nothing to do with racism whatsoever; it's all to do with overtime. If the corporation employs these people, it'll drastically reduce the overtime worked by the rest of the staff'.[10] Nevertheless, those 'coloured workers' did not perceive the strike in terms of 'overtime'. One Jamaican war veteran who had worked on the Wolverhampton buses was asked what he thought of the bus strike and he explained: 'They don't want coloured people. The busmen would like to get rid of all the coloured people. This 5% ruling just so that they can dodge the colour bar question. But they'd like to get the coloured people out – so would a good many people. The war is over, people have changed.'[11] In a short space of time the strike was resolved insofar as the workers went back to work and the Transport Committees in Wolverhampton and West Bromwich continued to employ black workers. The TGWU union secretary for the Wolverhampton buses insisted that the action had not been in relation to a 'colour bar' and explained: 'When our industry became attractive to all others but Englishmen we began to worry. We would have imposed a bar on anyone coming from countries where the working conditions were not quite as good as our own whether they were European or West Indian.' The union campaign had gained little traction as the secretary acknowledged: 'when we saw that the public was against us and when we saw this was a very unpopular move we withdrew our demand for a 5% bar'.[12]

The statement by the union represented a climbdown insofar as workers from the Commonwealth were permitted to continue working on the buses. But the very presence of Sikh workers and other 'coloured' workers within the workplace had, through the experience of 1955, been seriously challenged. Memories of the strike lingered, illustrating to these workers their precarious position. This was coupled with everyday racist abuse experienced during work. In a report by the journalist Dilip Hiro it was noted that assaults on 'coloured crews on late night buses' were endemic in Wolverhampton. For example, in January 1968 a group of white youths refused to pay a fare to the Caribbean conductor and, when he insisted, the youths attacked him as well as the Caribbean driver. None of the white passengers came to their aid, with the honourable exception of a fire brigade employee. Some did telephone the police, but the police arrived late and took no statements from the 'coloured crew', then or later.[13]

In this context, the two-year dispute on the Wolverhampton buses led by Sikh workers was a way of organising for acceptance and rights within the workplace on their own terms. It had been inspired not in an abstract religious awakening, but through local connections between different workplaces. In May 1967 a group of Sikhs had applied for work at the large Goodyear factory in Wolverhampton. They were turned away by management because of the turbans they wore. The employer's rejection made clear to the current Sikh workers within the factory that they were only passively accepted within tightly controlled rules from above. Mr Sandhu senior and other Sikh workers, all of whom were already employed within the factory, took the opportunity to fight the matter on their own behalf to get turbans accepted by company rules. They threatened that if the employers did not allow the turban they would walk out on strike, not only in Wolverhampton but also involving the workers in the Goodyear factories in the Punjab.[14] The management responded with a change of uniform, and the turban was then allowed to be worn at the Goodyear factory in Wolverhampton.[15]

Mr Sandhu senior had a son, Tarsem Singh Sandhu, who worked as a conductor on the Wolverhampton buses. In August 1967 Mr Sandhu junior returned to work after a period of absence, having now grown a beard and with a new demand that his faith be taken seriously within his place of work.[16] The successful workers' struggle at Goodyear that his father and others had led, in one of the largest workplaces in Wolverhampton, informed the actions of Tarsem Singh Sandhu. Sandhu junior recalled that he had initiated the dispute after long discussions with his father and his intention was to make his family proud.[17] This act of resistance was part of a working-class shared experience within the Sandhu family and no doubt other connections existed between Sikh workers at Goodyear and on the buses, two of the biggest employers of Commonwealth immigrants within the town. The Goodyear dispute was used as an important benchmark to judge the transport employers and from which those workers on the buses could learn. Those perceived as 'immigrant workers' were beginning to challenge the way the workplace was being run.

A vox pop of passengers on Wolverhampton buses taken at the start of the dispute revealed that the majority of those questioned had no objection to the beard or turban being worn by bus workers. Passengers responded with comments such as 'if they can wear them in their own country they can wear them here' and another responded simply and to the point that 'I would not object as long as we could get there and back'.[18] Nevertheless, Mr Sandhu's managers did not react with the same indifference. Instead, Mr Sandhu was sent home from work and then, following a meeting with Sikh representatives and the Transport Committee, he was sacked. The chairman of the Transport Committee noted that the rules of uniform could not be changed without employer and trade union agreement.

The struggle for the right to wear a turban and beard became an important means by which to challenge far greater structural inequalities within the workplace. In response to Mr Sandhu being sent home, a campaign in his defence was launched in Wolverhampton, taken up by the Akali Dal, an Indian political Sikh organisation, as well as the very active local Indian Workers' Association, who began to lobby MPs for help. It was agreed by the Transport Committee that they would defer a final decision on the matter until they had heard from the TGWU union. The union finally agreed to discuss the matter after the Sikhs who were employed in the department threatened to form their own union. At the next union branch meeting, the Sikh workers turned out in force, and the question of changing the regulations was discussed. The secretary of the union, a full-time official, said that no final decision could be made at that meeting and instead the matter should be decided by a ballot of all the unionised staff. This was a highly unusual response. Even so, at the end of September 1967 the question was put to trade union members on the buses and the question on the ballot read: 'Are you in favour of ex-driver Sandhu's request to wear a beard and turban?' Out of 900 or more employees, 578 voted. The result was a majority in favour of the request: 336 for, 204 against, 38 spoiled ballot papers. It seemed a decision had been made by the workers themselves, yet it was a result which came as a great surprise to the union officials who had organised the ballot and had evidently expected a vote against Sandhu's request.[19] Bus workers took a clear anti-racist position, with a majority making their voices heard that Sikh workers should have a right to wear a turban and beard.

Despite the result of the ballot, the dispute continued. At the beginning of November, the city's Transport Committee met to consider the union request for a change. The committee, comprising both Conservative and Labour members, voted unanimously that Mr Sandhu could not work with a beard or a turban, rejecting the proposed change. The ban was justified by the Transport Committee with the insistence that all employees were to be treated alike. Yet as John Kassie, liaison officer for Wolverhampton Council for Racial Harmony pointed out, more than half of the bus crews were 'coloured', 100 had been employed for more than six years, but as yet not one held a supervisory post.[20] It was evident that not all employees were treated alike.

A national march was then called in Wolverhampton in February of 1968 in protest at the decision. Between 5,000 and 6,000 protestors attended, mainly Sikhs from across the country but also people from left-wing groups and the Council of Churches, with banners appealing for religious freedom. This was the largest political protest in Wolverhampton since the war, the march stretching for more than a mile.[21] In his Walsall speech soon after, Powell described the campaign as 'communalism', a 'curse of India' now rearing its head in Wolverhampton.[22] Two months later Powell made his 'Rivers of Blood' speech, and the turban dispute was again mentioned within it. He described the dispute in terms of 'acting against integration', and talked of vested interests sharpening racial and religious differences 'with a view to the exercise of actual domination'.[23] Powell's concern that immigrant workers were beginning to organise also coincided with a memory of a past Empire. The 'curse of India', a country Powell had once dreamed of ruling, was shaped by a history of decolonisation. For Powell, such a history of resistance could not be allowed to travel into the dynamics of struggle within the British working class.

Powell's speeches pushed the dispute into the national spotlight, but the Sikh workers refused to back down. In the last month there was even a threat of suicide if the decision was not changed; 'Mr Joly he said he was going to burn himself in front of the civic hall if they did not change their mind' one of the Sikh bus drivers recalled.[24] Finally, on 9 April 1969 and under pressure from national government, the Transport Committee met and agreed to change the turban rule for bus staff. In their announcement to the press, they made clear that this had not been a choice they agreed with. Acknowledging the change in regulations, the statement went on to note that 'the committee remains strongly of the view that its original decision was right, its rule both reasonable and clearly non-discriminatory'.[25] Chairman of the Transport Committee, Alderman Ronald Gough, explained: 'We feel we have been pressured.' He added: 'Of course we are alive to the fact that other racial minority groups might seek to put pressure on the council for their own ends.'[26] In this sense, the success of the Sikh bus workers came from the activities of the workers themselves and was never given or even accepted by their employers. Mr Bahra was part of the dispute, supporting his friend from the Gurdwara who worked on the buses and he joined the protests opposing the ban. When employers changed their position he decided to start work on the buses as he could now express his religion while working.[27] It seemed, also, to change the feelings between the bus workers themselves, with a confidence given to all workers to challenge the rules of their employers, as the Transport Committee themselves acknowledged. One white bus conductor, who arrived just after the dispute, recalled how pleased the majority of bus workers were at the result.[28] The dispute had asserted a right to be treated as equals within the workforce, in respect of their own traditions, and served as a delayed resistance to the racism they had been forced to endure over their very presence as workers on the buses of Wolverhampton. It could give confidence to all racial minorities organising for their rights within the workplace.[29] In this vein the dispute does not have to be read as a kind of sectarian form of self-interest, but actually opened up a wider attack on management control of workers, allowing other workers to assert their rights. It was this struggle and the potential in spreading much more widely that perhaps most worried Powell.

'Inside out and upside down': Enoch Powell and the young

The bus workers were not the only ones targeted in Powell's speeches in 1968. Powell's focus on the buses reflected the needs of employers as they attempted to push divisions within the workforce. Yet in reality Wolverhampton had very high employment rates in the 1960s as the town continued its economic boom. In contrast, shortages in school places were a major focus of popular resentment in the area, which Powell could more successfully invoke through the prism of race. Those who had moved to Wolverhampton for work also had children of school age, some of whom were brought over and others born in Britain. In itself, this simple fact became cause for alarm. There were both too many of these 'immigrant children' attending local schools, as well as not enough.

In 1950s Wolverhampton the stories focused on the 'tragedy of the lost children' where chance visits by welfare workers to the homes of Pakistani and Indian immigrants uncovered 'lost children' who were not even on school lists.[30] At the same time, much of the local reporting of 'immigrant children' focused on their role in occupying and overcrowding the schools of Wolverhampton. In language that was framed by racial warfare, these children became the physical proof of immigrant fertility, an enemy multiplying rapidly waiting to destroy the peace of white England from within. That they appeared as innocent and sweet could prove all the more provocative as a cover for this takeover. They were no longer simply children, but were instead intently observed as an 'immigrant problem' through which a crisis of education in Wolverhampton had been created. In this vein, measuring ratios between what was interchangeably described as that of 'whites and coloureds' or 'whites and immigrants' became an accepted part of educational discourse.

Yet, just as in employment, schools in Wolverhampton were also sites where a racist ideology could become less real on an everyday level. Black and white children now shared the same teachers, playgrounds and even friendships. In contrast to the narrative of immigrant children taking over, the young also started to be identified as a source of interracial harmony, acting as a kind of custodian for integration. There were dozens of reports on the successes of these new spaces in Wolverhampton where children from different racial backgrounds were brought together. Deploying a somewhat simple approach of inviting all children within the area to attend, the running of these projects often unconsciously began to intervene in heated debates on immigration within the town. For example, a named 'multi-racial play group' initiated in 1968 was run by a white woman, Mrs Beryl Wheal of Wolverhampton, with 'the help of three Asian girls'. Mrs Wheal had been 'stopping turbaned gentlemen in the streets around the Len Road area and asking them if they have any children between the ages of three and five'. It was added by the reporter that while this may sound strange, it was one woman's attempts to help parents – whether English or immigrants – in the area.[31] These 'multiracial' projects became spaces in which an experimental belief in a future multicultural promise could be tested.[32]

There were thus conflicting positions on the role of 'immigrant children' in Wolverhampton schools. That education became such a heated site in which to debate the question of 'immigration' was also tied into revolts taking place globally in 1968 discussed in chapter 1. Student resistance was anxiously observed by educational figures in Wolverhampton. Riots in the Olympic city of Mexico City became headline news in the local paper, as thousands of students marched outside the stadium against the military occupation of their university. Reports of German and French student protests of 1968 were also front-page news in Wolverhampton. The fear of contagion was palpable as student struggles began to erupt within the British higher education system. The post-war boom had seen universities that were previously the training ground of the elite expand and open up to middle- and working-class students. Mr Howard was the headmaster of the elite boarding school of Royal Wolverhampton and, like many local education figures, called for urgent containment before student revolts developed further. Warning parents of the increasing dangers of the radicalised British university, Mr Howard outlined his fears that the role of education was becoming more and more distant from the needs and desires of employers. Mr Howard rooted the problem of student unrest within the rapid increase in the size of universities as well as the 'sudden dramatic increase in social science faculties' that were not attracting the 'best boys'. In fact, disciplinary 'true standards' had apparently fallen to such worrying levels that Mr Howard stressed that his school would direct itself away from universities.[33] The headteacher's fearful warnings illuminated the instabilities within education as students began to challenge the very meaning of that system.

The figure of the 'immigrant child' was born out of and became one way in which to focus on wider educational anxieties in this period. Panics developed around the numbers of these children, their assumed lower standards and cultural differences and how this would impact on the remaining white students. Of course, just like the 'immigrant' workers on the buses, the definition of an 'immigrant child' was hard to pin down. The 'immigrant child' often stood in for coded debates on black children, and before 1966 there were no guidelines on the definition of an 'immigrant child'. Indeed, as one journalist sent to the town following the speech noted: 'There are more Italian children in the primary schools than there are Pakistanis. No one is objecting to their presence anymore.'[34] From 1966 until 1972 the government Department of Education and Science collected data to get a sense of the 'immigrant' school population, and within this exercise an 'immigrant child' was defined as someone either born outside the UK or someone who was actually born in the UK to parents who had been in the country less than ten years.[35] Statistics collected on 'immigrant children' intertwined with an educational policy framed around the burden they placed upon schools. From 1964 onwards central government policies recommended to local education authorities that 'immigrant pupils' (undefined at the time policy was initiated) should be dispersed with a commitment to the view that the proportion of immigrants in any school or class should not rise above one-third, that the catchment areas of schools might be adjusted to ensure this, and that 'bussing' immigrants to schools out of their neighbourhood might be similarly used. The idea of limiting the proportion of 'immigrant children' in a school was drawn from a report of the Commonwealth Immigration Advisory Council, published in early 1964, which stated:

> The presence of a high proportion of immigrant children in one class slows down the general routine of working and hampers the

work of the whole class, especially where the immigrants do not speak or write English fluently. This is clearly in itself undesirable and unfair to all the children in the class. There is a further danger that educational backwardness which, in fact, is due to environment, language or a different culture may increasingly be supposed to arise from some inherent or genetic inferiority ... The evidence we have received strongly suggests that if a school has more than a certain percentage of immigrant children among its pupils the whole character and ethos of the school is altered.[36]

The racial suspicion towards such children was evident, and it was stressed that to truly integrate such children they would need to be spread out to prevent such educational 'backwardness'. Following the election of a Labour government in 1964, dispersal continued to be recommended as policy, although of course it was only the immigrant children who would be 'bussed out', rather than the white children also 'bussed in'. The government stated: 'As the proportion of immigrant children in a school or class increases the problems will become more difficult to solve, and the chances of assimilation more remote.'[37] Education policy in this period was thus framed around fears of a black concentrated majority with the white child dying out, imagined as a kind of inverse racial nightmare.[38]

In this sense, Powell's new focus on immigrant children was not drawn from thin air, nor was it a complete aberration from mainstream politics. For Powell, education became a key site in which to frame his new anti-immigrant politics in his attempts to stretch the boundaries of this discourse. Unlike government education policy, however, Powell insisted these 'immigrant children' could never become British despite knowing no other home, stating that 'the West Indian or Asian does not, by being born in England, become an Englishman'.[39] From this position, Powell argued that the numbers of these outsiders within the English education system was creating a national crisis. These themes crystallised in Powell's Walsall speech of February 1968. This was a speech which attempted to capture the 'sense of hopelessness and helplessness' which had come over those in Walsall and Wolverhampton in the face of 'continued flow of immigration into our towns'. Shortages of school education places were directly linked with the 'continuing influx of immigrants' while Powell clarified that most of these immigrants were 'children of school age or below'. These feelings of despair were given symbolic form through the image of the lone white child:

> Only this week a colleague of mine in the House of Commons was dumbfounded when I told him of a constituent whose little daughter was now the only white child in her class at school. He looked at me as if I were a Member of Parliament for central Africa, who had suddenly dropped from the sky into Westminster. So far as most people in the British Isles are concerned, you and I might as well be living in central Africa for all they know about our circumstances.[40]

Powell's focus on immigrant children taking over the schools in his own constituency would emerge again in his 'Rivers of Blood' speech. The speeches pushed both the Wolverhampton education system and those 'immigrant children' into the national spotlight. Drawn in by Powell's words, the media began a hunt for such 'immigrant schools' of Wolverhampton. A series of reports emerged on the peculiar ways of immigrant children and the associated 'crisis in schools'. One local report revealed the 'startling disclosure' that twenty-two immigrant children at one of Wolverhampton's 'overcrowded primary schools' had all come from the same address and this apparently summed up 'the magnitude of the town's immigrant problem'.[41] An article in the *Times* centred on the problems of the 'immigration situation' and particularly the problems of education within the town. It was claimed that within Wolverhampton schools all the 'standard norms' had now been 'turned inside out and upside down' by the continued arrival in the town of 'immigrant children'.[42] Similarly, the *Observer* argued that the schools of Wolverhampton, badly overcrowded and understaffed, had helped give the white community the impression that they were becoming 'strangers in their own land'. Twenty-three of the schools in the town, according to this report, had a percentage of 'immigrant publics' that was over the government's idea of a third, while ten of those schools were '50 per cent coloured'.[43]

However, much to the frustration of the press the lone 'white child' that Powell had talked of in his Walsall speech could not be found in any of the classes or schools of Wolverhampton. Mr Bailey, of the Wolverhampton branch of the National Union of Teachers, argued that no school existed with only one white child in a class. It was perhaps not a surprise then that Powell refused to identify the school when questioned.[44] Despite the lack of the singular white child, the media were not deterred. Instead, the press settled for West Park primary school as an example of an 'immigrant school' with a high percentage of 'immigrant children'. It began to be described as 'that 82% school' since apparently 240 pupils at the primary school were 'coloured'. The local paper noted: 'Whether West Park was Mr Powell's school with a class with only one white child – and there has been no official confirmation that it was – is now an academic point.'[45]

Yet the headteacher of the school, Mrs Eileen Llewellin-Davies, was outspoken in rejecting the attacks on West Park primary school. She pointed out the school in reality only had '40 immigrant children', while the rest were 'British-born and proud of it'.[46] In other words, as one local activist put it, the children were as English as Enoch Powell and spoke with the same accent as any others born and bred in the area. They were able to learn as rapidly as those whose skins were white.[47] In reporting to the governors, Eileen Llewellin-Davies noted that the school had become a 'centre of interest' for a large share of visitors, with Mr Lines, the education director of the town, bringing with him visitors from the Department of Education and Science, as well as reporters from ITV and the BBC.[48] In a TV report on the school less than two weeks after Powell's speech in Walsall, Eileen Llewellin-Davies was interviewed. In front of the children, the interviewer asked: 'Most schools like to keep a ratio between immigrant children and white children, presumably that's gone by the board here has it?' The headteacher responded that unfortunately it had, as there had been so many children arriving in such a short time and so the ratio had risen very quickly. While aware of the Education Ministry advice that the ratio shouldn't be any more than one-third to two-thirds, the teacher explained that in her school they were well above that ratio. Apparently 'neither side' was getting a fair deal although she concluded that they loved all of the children very much. Meanwhile the children continued their PE class in the background of the interview, seemingly unaware of the discussion on 'ratios' and 'sides'.[49] The curiosity around the school continued, with a report to governors acknowledging that the school was still receiving a steady flow of visitors, including the High Commissioner of India, an editor of the *Times*, two 'very charming' Swedish reporters and some 'not so charming' American reporters who were doing a survey of the 'immigrant problem' in the town. By June 1968 the school was attempting to halt the visits, and the *Daily Mail*, ITV and the BBC received little cooperation from the school as they felt they should 'attempt to turn the limelight away from us'.[50] The headteacher noted that 'Unfortunately, much adverse criticism has been reflected on this school during the past year'.[51]

Michael Edwards was a white child at West Park school and recalls the photographers and journalists turning up and positioning him and his black friends in photo shoots. The family joke was that Michael Edwards was the 'only white child' Powell had referred to, although it was clearly known within the family that this was not true, not least because, as he puts it, coming from an Irish family Michael had numerous white cousins who also attended the same school.[52] However, the press interest in the white child amongst immigrants would circulate across the world. A photograph of Michael taken with his black friend Ray in the school in February was then published in the Jamaican newspaper the *Sunday Gleaner* one day after Powell's 'Rivers of Blood' speech. The caption, written by staff at the Central Office of Information in London, celebrated the 'firm foundation for mutual understanding' which was being provided for immigrant children in this Wolverhampton school by bringing them up with a high standard of education and 'alongside British pupils through every aspect of life at the school'.[53] Educational figures in Wolverhampton disagreed, and responding to the article they pulled West Park primary school back into heated debates over the 'wrong impressions' given of Wolverhampton. The town's director of education, Mr G.W.R. Lines, announced his outrage that such a positive description of a Wolverhampton school had been sent out to those in Jamaica. Mr Lines described the photographs and the article as 'singularly misleading' and said that he would be writing to the Department of Education and Science drawing attention to the matter over the publicity. Mr Lines said: 'I intend to tell the Department of Education and Science that it would be unfortunate if this left the impression that Wolverhampton was full of ideally integrated schools like West Park when, in fact, we have serious problems of accommodation.'[54]

The educational department were therefore intent on making clear that new immigrants, especially children, were not welcome in the town. Within this hostile climate some of the white mothers of West Park primary began to protest, and it was reported that they had 'besieged the school' to demand 'greater dispersal of immigrants'. They claimed that their children were being 'outnumbered' four to one. Mrs Llewellin-Davies, the headteacher, was firm in reasoning with the mothers, and patiently rejected the claim that their children's education was suffering as a result of 'immigrant children'. She pointed out that there was a specialised teacher on her staff to deal with immigrants, and could not understand the objection of the mother who complained about a Jamaican folk song being included in a carol concert at the school. 'Why not?' she asked. 'I bet a lot of people have sung Way Down Upon the Swanee River when they were at school.' Mrs Llewellin-Davies concluded that they were very proud of all the children in the school and that 'we have a lot to learn from these children'.[55] The headteacher wrote in her report to governors that they had assured parents that their children were not suffering because of immigrants and that they had left, they had hoped, satisfied.[56] This did not, however, quell some of the white parents who had visited her to complain. Walking out of the meeting, one of the mothers, Mrs Phyllis Griffiths, explained to the press: 'You get the feeling that you are banging your head against a brick wall. We are dissatisfied, but what can we do?' Another companion suggested 'We could go and see Enoch'.[57]

Despite these tensions, school students' memories of their time at West Park primary were overwhelmingly positive ones. The photograph of Michael and Ray that had been published in the Jamaican press would be recaptured fifty years later at a reunion Michael organised with his school friends. They had very different memories of the school, where instead of 'problems' they talked of friendship and unity.[58] Angela Spence was a child in the school, and she recalled that the image of the lone white child was a 'blatant misrepresentation'. She explained:

> the school was diverse even then with a mix of children learning and playing together. Jackie and Susan, two white girls, were among my friends. I am the eldest of five children and we all went to West Park. We lived very locally in a house purchased by my parents in 1963, in a street with families from Fiji, Poland, South East Asia, the Indian sub-continent, Italy, Jamaica, Barbados, Monserrat and the United Kingdom. I enjoyed my school days.[59]

Outside of West Park primary school, however, there was a shortage in school places in particular areas of Wolverhampton. Mr Lines acknowledged that dispersal was used to respond to these shortages, although he was keen to stress the 'bussing' of these children was not in response to racial educational guidelines as it was done in other education boroughs. In 1968, thirteen buses distributed 550 children from Wolverhampton to about forty schools where places were available. Mr Lines argued that a 'fair number' of those 550 children were white, although in fact, as the *Observer* noted, 538 of them were 'coloured'. Moreover, it was the 'coloured children' who were on the waiting lists in schools, with practically all of those 400 children on the list non-white.[60] Meanwhile, Mrs Jan, one of the first Asian teachers in the town, recalls working in her first school, Bingley Road primary school, where she was forced to endure the racism of the headmistress. When Asian parents attempted to enrol their children in the school the headmistress would simply say there was not enough space, while she witnessed the headmistress allowing white children into the school. It was only when the educational office intervened that the headmistress would be forced to enrol such children. Mrs Jan complained about her own treatment and was transferred to Dudley Road primary school, where, instead, she was treated with respect by the children and management of the school.[61] There were then serious questions brought up on the racial distribution of students, with those classed as 'immigrant children' forced to endure bussing to schools far away from their homes and less likely to be accepted in schools nearby. Patrick Vernon's early education was one example of this. His parents migrated from Jamaica, with his dad arriving in Wolverhampton in 1958 and his mum the year after. Patrick was born and lived in Wolverhampton as a child. But in his first months attending primary school he had to travel out of Wolverhampton, and his mum remembers taking him to get a coach which would then drive him to his primary school in Tipton.[62]

In response to these school shortages and the bussing of children, Grove primary school was launched in Wolverhampton. Patrick stopped having to be bussed to school outside Wolverhampton and instead could attend his new local primary from September 1968. The headteacher of Grove primary, Mr Ernest Rhoden, explained how the school had been opened in response to the problem of having to find 320 extra school places very quickly, and it had taken just four months to build the new 'instant' school.[63] Meanwhile the local paper had already begun to describe the school as holding '90% immigrant pupils' although of course such a definition ultimately meant non-white children.[64] The national press similarly reported on the school and the 239 children, of whom only forty were white.[65] That the school had such large numbers of non-white students could be explained by the fact that the majority of the classes of the 250 children attending had been transferred from seventeen other schools and that in the past they have been ferried across the town in special buses.[66]

On the opening of Grove primary school a local TV report showed the headmaster rounding up his pupils for a register. 'If I do not pronounce your name properly, remember your name is probably as strange to me as mine is to you', Mr Rhoden told the children. The local paper dramatically concluded that 'day one at Grove, the most publicised school in the West Midlands, has begun'. Among the parents who had come to see their children start at the school were a 'handful of white fathers and mothers' among the large crowd of mainly Caribbean and Asian parents. The father of one white child commented to the press: 'It's not integration, it is saturation.'[67] In response to such mutterings, framed as they were by Powell's speeches on the topic, the headteacher insisted that no white child would be left alone in a class. Indeed the headteacher went so far as to rearrange the classes to provide one class with an equal number of 'white and coloured children'. This arrangement meant that children were moved between years so that white children would be placed within the same class despite their age differences. Mr Rhoden explained that fifteen white children in one of the three first-year classes had been put with fourteen 'coloured' children. The other two first-year classes were wholly 'immigrant'.[68] The vision of the lone white child was therefore actively prevented from becoming reality, to such an extent that whole classes were rearranged. This did not stop Powell from drawing the school into further national speeches and in his Eastbourne speech he denounced the 90 per cent 'immigrant school' in his own constituency.[69] Despite this, Powell was later invited to the official opening ceremony of the school by the headteacher, while a school governor and councillor, John Bird, refused to attend the ceremony because of the presence of Powell.[70] Similarly, there was disquiet from parents at this particular invitation and leaflets were distributed, in Punjabi and English, which 'called on immigrant parents to keep their children away because of Mr Powell's presence'.[71]

Despite the clear panic which surrounded the issue of 'immigrant children', by no means were these same children simply passive victims. The older generation of immigrants were often held back through fear of losing out on money, housing and jobs, yet it was observed that the young were ready to 'hit back' in Wolverhampton. Dilip Hiro noted, after spending time in the town, that there were 'great reserves of protest energy among coloured children' and their mood was unmistakably militant. Reported anecdotes gave a sense of this everyday resistance. When a Caribbean girl in secondary school was called a 'little monkey' by her white teacher in Wolverhampton, the girl hit him back – hard. Similarly, Rainforth Nelson, a young Jamaican, told the journalist: 'If a young coloured hears "black bastard" from a moving car he throws anything he can find at the car. He's not afraid anymore.' Moreover, it was observed that 'coloured youths' were especially sensitive to the post-Powell atmosphere in Wolverhampton. They pointed to the curious logic by which the word 'immigrant' had come to be used where 'coloured' was meant, often describing those children as 'immigrants' when many of them were born in this country. Young people were beginning to ask: How can you be an immigrant in a country where you were born?[72]

Powell's words of 1968 were therefore a response to changing dynamics within the fields of education and work within the town. The turban dispute, in particular, had demonstrated an immigrant grouping refusing to simply accept the discriminatory rules of their employers. Here, Powell's intervention could not quell the rising tide of anti-racist workplace organising in the context of full employment. In the town's overflowing school system, by contrast, Powell's speeches clearly had a greater impact – to such an extent that classes were racially rearranged to deny the press the image of the 'lone white child'. Powell's idea of an occupying enemy expanding in the town seeped into the ways in which schools were organised, as a sort of early prevention attempt. In this sense, Powell's focus demonstrated an ability to latch onto situations of real social inequalities and exploit these through the prism of race.

Yet his words also intensified the demands and struggles of those targeted within the speech. It became increasingly clear that anti-racism would have to be something organised and fought for, and particularly for the young, questions were brought out into the open on their place within Wolverhampton and indeed British society. These were questions that were left unresolved, and yet in pushing these tensions in different forms, black residents within the town were beginning to assert their rights to be treated not as a separate cultural problem but as a key part of the Wolverhampton working class.

5

A 'monstrous reputation': remembering Enoch Powell

All political lives, unless they are cut off in midstream at some happy juncture, end in failure.[1]

The intensity of defeat was experienced no more so than in the life of Enoch Powell. In 1968 Powell confided to his long-term friend, Clement Jones, the editor of the local newspaper the *Express and Star*: 'I'm going to make a speech at the weekend and it's going to go up "fizz" like a rocket', adding, 'but whereas all rockets fall to the earth, this one is going to stay up'.[2] The 'Rivers of Blood' speech did indeed serve as a rocket with all the fizz and excitement Powell had carefully planned. Yet the rocket did not stay up. By 1970 Heath had been elected prime minister of Britain and Powell was left severely isolated within his own party. Meanwhile the pockets of workers' support displayed for Powell had now dissipated. Instead workers' action had transformed into concerted trade union struggle. Such strike action often brought a multiracial working class together. On the buses, for example, a wave of strikes saw black and white drivers on the picket lines together.[3] Surjit Singh Sandhu, after almost ten years of working on the Wolverhampton buses, in the late 1970s became a shop steward for the trade union. Powell's vision of a white victim and an immigrant enemy was often challenged by the realities of work and changes within the trade union movement.

An organised fascist who had worked in the meat market, explained the walk out there in support of Powell following the speech: 'it was just that mood of the moment – like storming the Bastille I suppose', admitting that it was a mood which lasted no longer than a few weeks.[4] Yet the ideas of Powell were also pushed in new directions. A small fascist organisation, the National Front, had prominently taken up Powell's words in organisational form. 'Enoch is right' became their rallying call. In this sense the 'Rivers of Blood' speech allowed the National Front to bring the language and arguments of the fascist political fringe into the heart of the establishment.[5]

Simultaneously, the immigrants that Powell had talked of in such negative terms were also developing a newfound confidence in Britain. By 1969 one of the pioneers of ska music, Laurel Aitken, released a track in Britain titled 'Run Powell Run'. In 1970, the Jamaican singer Millie Small, who had achieved Britain's first ska number one with 'My Boy Lollipop', released a protest song on Trojan Records called 'Enoch Power'. It was subsequently banned by the BBC. Nevertheless, both tracks pointed to a new generation of black voices who refused to be cowed by the politics of Powell. In 1973 a TV interviewer inquired: 'many people are asking where does Enoch Powell go from here?' With little chance of a future Cabinet position, the interviewer accused Powell of being a 'voice in the wilderness' to which Powell nimbly responded that the wilderness was a good place for voices to reverberate.[6] Powell shocked many in 1974 when he stood down as MP. Instead, he called for a national vote for Labour, in opposition to Conservative support for the European Common Market. Abandoning his constituency of Wolverhampton, Powell moved to Northern Ireland to be elected MP in the South Down seat, representing the Ulster Unionists in the snap election of October 1974. Despite the retreat, the politics Powell had unleashed still lingered within Britain. In 1976 the musician Eric Clapton declared to a huge audience in Birmingham that Enoch Powell was right and there were too many foreigners in the country. 'Send them back' he shouted to the crowd, 'keep Britain white!' The outburst by Clapton illuminated the growing influence of the National Front and spurred on the birth of Rock against Racism in 1976. The carnivals and protests that followed, with the Clash, Buzzcocks and hundreds of local groups and activities across the country, were all part of a mass anti-racist movement which defiantly challenged the parameters and legitimacy of a new racism Powellism was attempting to strengthen and widen.[7]

Thatcher, however, pulled the particular anti-immigrant politics of Powell back into the mainstream when, in the run-up to the general election, she commented on the fears of the British people that the country might be 'rather swamped by people with a different culture'. Thatcher added 'So, if you want good race relations, you have got to allay people's fears on numbers'. These immigrants were carefully highlighted as those from 'the new Commonwealth and Pakistan'.[8] Those magical connections between race, the nation and immigration restrictions that Powell had developed were now being drawn upon by Thatcher. Moreover, Powell's earlier critique of Heath's Keynesian economic policies was now taken up under a new Thatcher government. It was this 'rich mix' (as Hall put it) that Powell had pioneered, economic liberalism in combination with tradition themes of nation, family, authority and race, that became Thatcherism.[9] It was not coincidental that Powell remained a reference point for Thatcher and was heard to refer to him privately as 'that golden-hearted Enoch'.[10]

Despite this influence, Powell remained a representative for the Ulster Unionists for much of Thatcher's rule. Powell was still conceived of as somewhat embarrassing by Conservative former colleagues and was forced to survive outside the political mainstream. In this respect, the anti-racist movement in Britain was successful. When Powell lost his seat in 1987, his exile from mainstream British politics seemed complete and, while there were rumours of Powell receiving some form of peerage by Thatcher, it did not materialise. Powell would never again receive the same attention and he was left a dwindling figure ruminating on the significance of failure. He referred to himself as 'dead' in political terms.[11]

Since his death in 1998, memories of Powell have been partial yet persistent and forever associated with his 'Rivers of Blood' speech. As Gilroy notes, it is a peculiar feature of race politics that many of the most powerful, influential people and institutions in Britain cannot leave the memory of Powell alone.[12] Each year on 20 April, the anniversary of this speech, there are renewed efforts to canonise Powell. Many of those who attempt this canonisation of Powell suggest, however, that his legacy must be detangled from a politics of race. 'Erudite, scholarly, a poet and philosopher, a brigadier in the army during the war and prominent politician, there is much to celebrate in Powell's life and work', one journalist tells us.[13] Supporters attempt to draw out a more multifaceted Powell; he proposed reform in the House of Lords while he also condemned the Conservative cover-up of the Hola Camp Massacre. There was 'exceptional integrity to the man', with Oborne writing of the need to remove the 'ugly background' that surrounds Powell.[14] Within these accounts there is an attempt to de-racialise the politics of Powell. Many of Powell's quotes are now seen as slightly distasteful reflections of the time, but irrelevant to his overall politics. Instead, invoking Powell is often used as a signifier in more coded debates as a politics that was first able to establish 'magical connections' and 'short-circuits' between the themes of race and immigration control, while evoking the images of the nation, the British people and the destruction of 'our culture, our way of life'.[15] Tracing the genealogy of these memories allows us to analyse the continuities, fissures and contradictions of racism as an ideology which has coalesced around the symbolism of Powell. The rest of the chapter examines the survival processes of Powell's memory and his partial rehabilitation from the wilderness.

Death

Powell often discussed his own death. Although in his later years Powell was pushed away from public sight and removed from mainstream politics he continued to work on preserving his views in history, publishing his own speeches and writings, and preparing his papers to allow others to write biographies of him. Powell was also keen to present an image of himself as a lone voice speaking out, a man who would go down in history, a prophet yet an outcast, as his biographer put it.[16]

On the radio show Desert Island Discs in 1989 Powell was asked by the interviewer how he would like to be remembered. 'Others will remember me as they will remember me' Powell responded before finally adding: 'I should like to have been killed in the war.'[17] The brigadier in uniform, fighting for his country, the man who had made a sacrifice for others, became central to Powell's invention of himself. The fighting soldier did not, in reality, correspond to Powell's experience of war, having been removed from combat. Similarly, in many interviews in later life Powell portrayed himself as the political equivalent of an oracle, a politician who has had a duty to speak the truth regardless of the consequences on his own career.[18] The myth of Powell's self-sacrifice for the national good would be a recurring one following his death. Of course, Powell did not die on the battlefields of war, but in 1998 aged eighty-five in a private London hospital.

Powell's funeral was carefully planned to project this image of sacrifice, as well as revealing significant connections that Powell had cultivated. In this sense, he was publicly mourned as both a national pillar within the establishment as well as an outsider from such networks. This ambiguity was reflected in the route the coffin took. Before his funeral, Powell's coffin lay in state at Westminster Abbey in the Chapel of St Faith. A public row broke out on whether Powell should have been accorded the honour of lying, in state or otherwise, in such a shrine to British nationhood. The church insisted the honour had been provided because of Powell's personal links with the church, as a warden to an adjoining church, and had nothing to do with his national political career. Despite protests, Powell's coffin lay overnight in the abbey and would be blessed the following morning. Its location served as a testimony to Powell's relationship with powerful British institutions.[19] After receiving these honours from the Church of England, Powell's body was moved on to his two funerals which took place first in St Margaret's Church in London and then in Warwickshire. Before his death Powell had requested a military funeral and to be buried with the regiment he had been part of fifty years previously. Powell was buried dressed in his brigadier uniform and the coffin, draped with the flag of the Union Jack, and placed near to where ten soldiers, including three former members of the Royal Warwickshires, were also buried.[20] Here was the brigadier Powell remembered in all his wartime glory, separated from the murky world of his lengthy political life. Yet he would also be celebrated within the political world.

Now that one of the most 'brilliant' figures in British political life was dead, the *Telegraph* called for the adjournment of parliament and argued that Powell's wife should be given a peerage.[21] While neither suggestion was taken up, the obituaries that poured in displayed a public reverence for the once isolated man. This was reflected almost unanimously across the political spectrum and it was the prime minister, Tony Blair, who led the voices of mourning. Blair stated that 'however controversial' Powell's views were, 'he was one of the greatest figures of twentieth century British politics, gifted with a brilliant mind. However much we disagreed with many of his views, there was no doubting the strength of his convictions or their sincerity, or his tenacity in pursuing them, regardless of his own self-interest'.[22] Powell's sacrifice, bravely pursuing political ideas to the detriment of political career, neatly mirrored how Powell had asked to be remembered.

Blair was not the only politician to mourn Powell's death and a long list of prominent politicians all paid their respects. Baroness Thatcher stated that there would never be anybody else so 'compelling' as Enoch Powell, describing him as 'magnetic' and listening to his speeches as an unforgettable privilege. Powell 'was one of those rare people', she argued, 'who made a difference and whose moral compass led us in the right direction'. The Conservative leader, William Hague, while stating there were sometimes profound disagreements between his party and Powell, added that Powell's contribution had helped shape the history of both the Conservative Party and contemporary politics. He concluded with an insistence that Powell would not be forgotten.[23] At the funeral the 'old order' was in attendance; John Major, Lord Parkinson, Michael Howard, Peter Lilley, Michael Portillo, William Waldegrave, Nicholas Budgen, Alan Clark, Ann Widdecome and Sir John Nott were all present. Even Tony Benn was there to mourn his old parliamentary friend.[24] The unanimity was complete and everyone who wrote about Powell following his death was certain of one thing, Enoch Powell was not a racist. This was all very odd, Paul Foot noted in his obituary, because the most important thing by far about Enoch Powell was that he was a 'racist pig of the most despicable variety'.[25] In the funeral speech the Conservative peer Lord Biffen acknowledged these attacks when he spoke of the 'snakes and ladders' Powell had endured within his career. Nevertheless Powell had also achieved an influence on a scale which perhaps only history would come to recognise, Biffen concluded.[26]

'Detoxifying the conversation'

The lavish send-off suggested a deep, if uncomfortable, relationship between the heart of parliament and Enoch Powell. Nevertheless, Powell's name emerged infrequently in the immediate years that followed his death. It appeared that any explicit legacy would be of little significance. The National Front, having gained in strength in association with Powell's speech, was now long since defeated. The Conservatives were out of power and in disarray as they attempted to evolve out of the Thatcher years. They had no interest in returning to the delicate subject of Powell. Meanwhile the New Labour government steered well away from explicitly referring to the murky waters of Powell's past. Conversely, these were also years in which immigration controls continued to tighten and a demonisation of 'illegal immigrants' became the overwhelming consensus in British politics. All major parties agreed that immigration must be controlled with stricter legislation in order to protect British society. A language of 'skivers' and 'cheats' in association with the figure of the darkened asylum-seeker enemy became normalised in this period.[27] Even so, Powell's name remained an irrelevance within this context.

In 2001 'race' riots broke out in Oldham, Bradford and Burnley, provoked by fascists and the police. In response, the government-commissioned Cantle report argued that the towns showed a 'depth of polarisation' with segregated communities living 'a series of parallel lives'. The report warned that further violence was likely if the polarisation was not broken. Reflecting on this report a few years later, Cantle sketched a narrative of British race politics which originated with Enoch Powell's 'Rivers of Blood' speech. According to Cantle, the way that

Powell had approached the topic of immigration had meant that different ethnic minority communities refused to deal with the wider issues Powell had raised. From then onwards parallel lives had apparently become entrenched.[28] Powell thus reappeared within this state narrative as a symbolic origin, creating a date in which to trace back to the 'problems' of ethnic minority divisions. Even so the reference to Powell was still a distant footnote.

By 2005 a new politics was developing around a 'crisis in multiculturalism' and challenging 'establishment' ways of thinking on race. Powell's name began to emerge more frequently in these discussions. This was not led by the far right or even Conservative groupings, but instead emerged from a network of centrist political figures, many of whom were associated with the ruling New Labour government. The turn in focus was most prominently expressed by Trevor Phillips. While chairman of the Commission for Equalities and Human Rights in 2005 Phillips famously declared that Britain was 'sleepwalking' into segregation. He continued to publicly warn of an increasing 'race segregation' which would bring 'civil strife' and 'fire' to the streets of British society. There were murmurs within the press that Phillips was transforming into a new Enoch Powell.[29] Perhaps it was these media parallels which encouraged Phillips to theatrically delve further into Powell's past. On the fortieth anniversary of the 'Rivers of Blood' speech, Phillips returned to the hotel where Powell had once made his notorious speech. Phillips stressed that Powell's speech had made it virtually impossible for Britain to have a proper policy on immigration for nearly half a century. If Powell represented paralysis, Phillips clearly viewed his choreographed return to the site of origin as an attempt to move beyond this moment, allowing for a new dialogue on the 'immigration debate'. Phillips paid tribute to David Cameron for being the first Conservative leader to be able to talk about race and immigration by adopting a more reasonable tone; Cameron had, in Phillips eyes, been right to call for a debate addressing issues of overcrowding and pressure on public services.[30]

Phillips represented a key wing within New Labour and was by no means a lone voice. Debates on immigration, separation and the 'white working class' began to evolve and crystallise in this period. David

Goodhart best encapsulated this politics with his public calls for liberals to 'get their act together over immigration'. In an essay he wrote for *Prospect* magazine in 2004, entitled 'Too diverse?' Goodhart argued that sharing and solidarity now conflicted with mass immigration and diversity. This was what he called the 'progressive dilemma' and, as he wrote, 'to put it bluntly – most of us prefer our own kind'.[31] He was soon labelled a liberal Powellite, with the BBC asking 'Is this man the left's Enoch Powell?'[32] Goodhart insisted he was not, but continued his arguments for less immigration and more nationalism in his book in 2013 where he attempted to challenge what he argued were left-wing myths in support of immigration. While Powell's 'Rivers of Blood' speech was significant, in part for making it 'slightly indecent' to talk about immigration, Goodhart argued he was attempting to move beyond this moment in pursuing a much-needed conversation on immigration. Rather than silencing the issues Powell had raised, Goodhart argued they needed to be addressed in a more refined manner.

Despite these assurances of separation from Powell, the politics initiated by Goodhart, Phillips and others appeared to have the opposite effect. For it was in this period in Britain that Powell's legacy was brought back into the open in association with new forms of anti-immigrant politics within mainstream culture. This was illuminated in 2008 when the BBC broadcast a series provocatively entitled 'White Season'. The series intended to shine a spotlight on the 'white working class' in Britain, interrogating why some people felt 'under siege' and how their very sense of being had been 'brought into question'. To visualise this, the trailer for the series showed a number of brown hands scrawling messages in foreign languages upon the face of a balding white man. In the background Billy Bragg sings a call for the building of a New Jerusalem. Eventually the white man's face is covered in so much ink that he can no longer be seen against the black background.[33] Central to this series was the documentary 'Rivers of Blood' which attempted to understand the speech in a new light, reassembling the surviving fragments of the tape to recreate the whole speech. Powell's words are repeated over and over again in the film, while footage shows us the dockers marching in support of Powell, then the 1981 riots and finally 7/7 attacks and the wreckage of the London bus. At the start of the documentary, the narrator states: 'in the wake of riots and terror attacks, many are now asking, was Enoch Powell right to predict disaster in his "Rivers of Blood" speech?' These anonymous supporters of Powell reappear throughout the documentary in the narrator's voice, and the programme concludes that 'ten years after his death, many believe that Powell's arguments were often prescient'. We are left with no evidence or examples of who these many people believing in Powell are. As one historian noted, the programme seemed designed to suggest that Powell was right and that he was speaking up for the white working class who had been excluded from political debate.[34] The most glowing review of the documentary was given by the leader of the British National Party (BNP), Nick Griffin. He gloated that if the BNP had made a documentary on Powell 'it wouldn't have differed too much from this'.[35] The political ostracism that Powell had suffered was thus openly challenged in the documentary broadcast to the nation, with a more sympathetic mainstream account presented of the politician. Powell had been rediscovered.

There was now no holding back those who had first tentatively introduced Powell's name into wider discussions on immigration, race and ethnicity. By 2016, Powell was now not so much in the way, but rather a key figure within Phillips' developing argument, providing a guide for the language and metaphors deployed. Raging against the liberal elite, Phillips argued: 'We maintain a polite silence masked by noisily debated public fictions such as "multiculturalism" and "community cohesion".' 'Rome may not yet be in flames', he continued, 'but I think I can smell the smouldering whilst we hum to the music of liberal self-delusion'.[36] These were words which echoed those of Powell's, almost fifty years on, and the reverberations were not coincidental. Phillips explained that Powell too had summoned up echoes of Rome. The impact of Powell's speech, according to Phillips, was that 'Everyone in British public life learnt the lesson: adopt any strategy possible to avoid saying anything about race, ethnicity (and latterly religion and belief) that is not anodyne and platitudinous'. Phillips, however, intended to break the silence, calling for a frank and open discussion of the possibility of a link between rape and the perpetrators' 'cultural background'.[37] Powell was now not something to be ashamed of and there could be no shying away from those 'difficult conversations' that Powell had first initiated. Phillip's focus has therefore become one of speaking out, of saying the 'Things We Won't Say About Race That Are True' as the title for his Channel 4 programme put it.

Phillips has therefore done much work in the road to Powell's rehabilitation. Of course, Powell has always had his most ardent of supporters alongside this. Simon Heffer is the most vocal of these as Powell's biographer and friend, writing prolifically in defence of Powell and railing against his removal from mainstream politics. For other journalists in the *Telegraph*, having once mourned Powell's death, their interest has only emerged again more recently. In 2010 a journalist for the newspaper wrote a review of a TV series with the headline 'Enoch Powell was not an out-and-out racist'. The writer complained that it was almost as rare as a graceful tango from Ann Widdecombe to hear a 'good news story about Enoch Powell'. It was a 'regrettable consequence' of his infamous speech in 1968 that it 'overshadowed his other achievements'.[38] These complaints continued. By 2014 the Conservative politician Daniel Hannan was writing in the *Telegraph* that Powell's 'monstrous reputation' was hiding the real man who, on the two big issues of his day, was 'dead right'. It was therefore sad that what remained of Powell's legacy was a name with which to, if not quite frighten children, at least bludgeon opponents.[39] Dealing with this 'monstrous' legacy has therefore been an ongoing process by individuals and institutions intent on rehabilitating Powell's memory. Powell is now more of a household name than in 1998, having been introduced into mainstream discussion by voices that would not naturally have been thought of as his bedfellows. Even so, it would be wrong to presume that mainstream politicians are at ease with remembering him publicly. Within British parties, the relationship with Powell is complicated.

UKIP and Powell

2016 was the year of political revolution, in the words of UK Independence Party (UKIP) leader Nigel Farage, the year that changed everything.

Following the Brexit result of June 2016, in November of that year Donald Trump was elected president of the United States. Days after this shock result Farage met Trump, becoming the first British politician to meet the president-elect following the election victory. Farage tweeted a photograph of the two men smiling together in front of an opulent, golden door. The image went viral, and seemed to represent a new politics which had taken on a global form.

The same week Farage was invited to give a talk in Florida at the David Horrowitz Freedom Center's Restoration Weekend. His speech focused on Brexit, Trump and his own role in these new political times. Unconsciously paraphrasing Lenin, Farage spoke of decades when little happened, and occasionally a year in which decades could happen. Much of the speech focused on this new year of change, yet Farage also returned to 1968 to respond to a question on the life and career of Enoch Powell. Launching into a recital of a passage from the 'Rivers of Blood' speech, Farage apologised for failing to do justice to Powell's accent and then pronounced: 'Those whom the gods wish to destroy first they make mad.' In an attempt to update the speech in his own words, Farage continued: 'And we must indeed be mad to allow the unqualified flow of tens of thousands of migrants into Britain every single year.' For those within the audience who had not heard of Powell, a glowing overview was then provided; the youngest professor in the British Empire, also the youngest brigadier in the British army, never a career politician, quite like Farage in this sense apparently, 'the bloke was extraordinary in every way'. Farage did also discuss the tactical problems which had blighted Powell's career trajectory. It was important to be ahead of public opinion and the media, to be like a magnet to bring people with you. Yet there was a problem if you attempted to go too far ahead, to a place people were not ready to even conceive of. According to Farage, it was this failure which led to the destruction of Powell's career, 'without doubt, the most talented post-war politician in Britain'. This defeat allowed the liberal media elite 'to make immigration a banned subject', a period in which 'nobody with a sensible voice or view in British politics, dared to touch the subject' of immigration. It was only Farage himself, Farage argued, who had been able to break through the silence while standing on the shoulders of a publicly disgraced yet valiant Powell.[40]

Powell's influence had featured prominently in Farage's political journey and the formation of UKIP. In his autobiography, *Fighting Bull*, Farage described his early years studying at the elite private school of Dulwich. Powell visited the school to give a speech to the students and Farage recalled how he was 'dazzled' into an 'awestruck silence' by Powell's words.[41] In Farage's first foray into political organising, he chauffeured Enoch Powell to a meeting backing an independent candidate who was part of an embryonic UKIP. When they reached the event at Newbury racecourse they found a small crowd of 'communist demonstrators tipping paraffin over Union Jacks and setting them on fire' who began to attack the car. According to Farage, Powell was 'totally unmoved by the attack' and Farage remembered him going on to give a fiery, colourful, logical and persuasive speech. Despite his 'occasional errors', Farage insisted 'Brigadier Powell' was a singularly great man who had 'achieved so much and sacrificed so much for his principle'. His presence had awoken in Farage 'all sorts of aspirations in me which I had not even acknowledged before. It inspired me'.[42] Through these recollections, Farage situated himself as the true inheritor of Powell's legacy.

This relationship was powerfully brought into the open on national TV in 2014 when Farage was invited on to the BBC's 'Question Time'. The comedian and political activist Russell Brand turned to Farage and stated: 'he's a pound shop Enoch Powell, and we gotta watch him'. Farage offered neither a defence nor rejection of Powell, and instead was left struggling to respond to the accusation. The taunting words would be hard to remove. Nevertheless, the controversial nature of Enoch Powell was evident even within UKIP. In 2015 Douglas Carswell, the only MP for UKIP, wrote that Powell in his pessimism was wrong. Immigration had not been without its challenges, Carswell argued, however, it had overwhelmingly been a story of success.[43] Struggles over Powell's legacy therefore illuminated serious divisions within UKIP that would later deepen and split.

Mainstream politics and the 'underbelly'

The legacy of Powell has not taken the same central place within other political organisations in Britain, although in Conservative circles Powell's name has become a more regular feature. To refer to Powell almost always requires an obligatory prefix separating his more 'extremist' positions from their own political traditions. Of course, there are times when more minor Conservative figures are less nuanced in their outbursts. In 2007 Nigel Hastilow, the former editor of the *Birmingham Post*, was selected as the Conservative candidate for the Halesowen and Rowley Regis constituency in the Black Country. In his column for the *Express and Star* Hastilow argued that Powell was 'right' in his 'Rivers of Blood' speech. According to Hastilow, Powell had been marginalised politically for his speech although he was right in that immigration had dramatically changed the country for the worst. The candidate was forced to step down as Conservative parliamentary candidate, while the Labour Cabinet minister Peter Hain noted that 'this Conservative candidate really exposes the racist underbelly of the Tory party'.[44]

More recently, a Conservative councillor in Coventry told a fellow Conservative Party member that he 'didn't believe in multiculturalism' and that 'Enoch Powell was right' while also suggesting that non-English-speaking immigrants were 'taking over' the country and should 'go home'. Asked about the views expressed around Enoch Powell, he said: 'Enoch Powell is a great hero of mine. I think he was a very intelligent man, a very far-seeing man, a very well respected member of Parliament. People said Enoch Powell was a racialist, but he wasn't. He made it quite clear what he was saying was nothing to do with race, it is to do quite simply with the numbers in this country.'[45] These were statements which were far more direct in their support of Powell and came immediately following the European referendum result. Such a shift was too much for some within the party. Deliberating on the Brexit bill following the referendum, the Conservative MP Kenneth Clarke noted:

> I feel the spirit of the former colleague who I rather respected, apart from one or two of his extreme views, my former colleague Enoch

Powell. The best speaker of the Eurosceptic cause I've probably ever heard in this House of Commons. If he was here he probably would find it amazing to believe that his party had become Eurosceptic and rather mildly anti-immigrant in a really strange way in 2016. Well I'm afraid on that I haven't followed them and I don't intend to do so.[46]

Invoking Powell's spirit, Clarke was careful to stress his respect for his 'former colleague' and his abilities, while removing himself from 'one or two' of his views. Powell is instead situated as simply one wing within the party, a wing which has now, to Clarke's shock, taken dominance within his party. In a post-Brexit climate, it appeared that Powell's 'spirit' had returned. Powell was well known as a leading anti-Europeanist from a right-wing perspective and so a newfound interest in the ex-Conservative figure following the referendum result would be expected.[47] However, the turn to Powell was not simply framed by a right-wing Brexit position. The earlier section of this chapter has shown the roots of Powell's revival were also evident within liberal Britain. Moreover, following the referendum result the echoes of Powell could be heard within sections of the Labour Party that had campaigned most vigorously to remain within the European Union.

At the Labour Party conference of 2016 there was an uneasy tension. Corbyn's election as leader of the party signalled a change in direction. His leadership was fiercely opposed by the majority of Labour MPs and immigration policy became one key pole within this internal battle. Intervening on the question of immigration, the Labour MP Rachel Reeves argued that her party needed to 'wake up'. In the speech Reeves argued there were 'bubbling tensions in this country that I just think could explode' if immigration was not curbed after Brexit. Reeves noted that the reality of this inactivity could already be observed in her constituency of Leeds West. Since the referendum, there had been three alleged racist attacks in her constituency, which included the largely white and economically deprived areas of Armley and Bramley. The most serious of these came when a Polish man ended up in hospital after being assaulted by a group of twenty youths. To stop these attacks in future, Reeves urged her party to end freedom of movement in Europe and to tighten immigration controls. Removing the presence of immigrants, in Reeves' logic then, would both alleviate the fear immigrants had of racism, since presumably they would no longer remain within the country, while also meaning racists would have no need to act on their hostility. In her most dramatic line, Reeves stressed the urgency of further immigration controls, warning that her own constituency was 'like a tinderbox'. The selection of such incendiary words echoed those of Powell. In Reeves' violent prophecy, she was accused of 'channelling' Enoch Powell.[48] This was not an isolated intervention, but represented a section of the party, once dominant, who had made strict immigration controls a central component of Labour policies.

Yet Powellism had also begun to be explicitly challenged by opposing forces within the Labour Party. Diane Abbott, the shadow home secretary, recently explained in a speech on immigration how as a school girl she heard of the 'Rivers of Blood' speech:

> I wasn't following it in huge detail but I do remember how I felt. People were talking about it even in school and I felt frightened. I didn't quite know why, I didn't know exactly what had been said, but I felt frightened. And of course, one of the issues around immigration in some political quarters is that immigration is a euphemism for race, and you can't have a serious debate about immigration unless you are prepared to face up to that.[49]

The immigration policy of Labour was now ambiguous, but Abbott's speech marked an attempt to reorient it dramatically. It is curious that a very different memory of Powell was invoked within this speech to help give meaning to this new policy direction. Powell again emerged in the recent elections of 2017 when Eleanor Smith was elected as a new Labour MP for the seat of Wolverhampton South West. Smith is a trade unionist and nurse and the first African-Caribbean MP to represent the West Midlands. This was a swing seat which was viewed as a likely Conservative win. Instead, Smith won with a 6 per cent swing from the Labour incumbent who had won the seat in 2015. There was much political commentary on the fact that Smith had won in the former seat of Enoch Powell. Following her election victory, Smith explained: 'He [Powell] was making the speech when my parents and many others came to this country. Now we can actually put that to rest. Wolverhampton South West is a very mixed, diverse, multi-cultural community.'[50] In another interview Smith stated how her election, she felt, could close the chapter of Powell and the 'Rivers of Blood' speech for good.[51] Interestingly, Smith's win was in a city which had produced an unexpectedly high vote to leave the European Union, with 62 per cent of Wolverhampton voting in support of Brexit. It is also a city with a 36.5 per cent ethnic minority population. The two election results together suggest simply equating Brexit with a rise in Powellism is untenable in this case. A vote for Brexit did not directly translate into a vote for a Conservative representative more aligned with Powell's political past.

Instead, to truly reckon with the legacy of Powell means acknow-ledging the range of political voices who have drawn from the anti-immigration politics of this past. This is not simply a phenomenon of the far right, but has also been pushed by supposedly liberal voices, who have attempted to sanitise Powell's words, to translate them into more palatable, mainstream ones. This politics cannot rid itself of the racial divisions that Powell once formulated, and the chapter has demonstrated the indelible memories of Enoch Powell which are often invoked within such framings. Reviving the memory came as much from elements of liberal Britain as from the brazen admiration of Farage. Saying Powell's name was not always needed, but appeared unavoidable at other moments as a sort of periodic ritual in exposing the undercurrent realities of British politics. Remembering Powell is a process in which a cacophony of different voices have all emerged in protest at the invisible silence or taboo or banning of conversations they all argue exist. These invocations of Powell work as a device, however, in shutting down access to a more complex history of struggle and resistance of which Powell's speech was an important event.

Conclusion

T HIS BOOK HAS explored the emerging responses to Powell's 'Rivers of Blood' speech in the weeks and months that followed. In Wolverhampton in this period the momentum was with the Powellites, breaking through a stagnated British politics and creating new forms of racial divisions. There was, however, resistance to Powell within the town and the research has revealed a contested, local history in response to Powell's words. These responses were born out of everyday relations within the town but were urged on by the media spectacle that Powell's words had created. Such struggles lay the roots for future resistance in the 1970s. The bus dispute by Sikh workers, for example, had by 1974 opened up new spaces through which women were now demanding that they be hired and treated with the same respect within this workforce.[1] Similarly, anti-racism soon took on a more organised form. In 1976 the Wolverhampton Anti-Racism Committee was initiated to oppose the National Front and the racism that had permeated the area.[2] Rock against Racism and later the Anti-Nazi League, both locally and nationally, were also part of creating a mass movement that pushed the fascists back. In 1978 thousands of Wolverhampton people marched against the racist violence of the National Front.[3] This anti-racist movement spread out into all aspects of society. One expression of this was the Black Art Movement formed in 1979, a group of black artists, many of whom were from Wolverhampton, culturally reflecting on where they existed in the uncertainty of the times. Their first exhibition of 1981 at the Wolverhampton Art Gallery was instigated by Eric Pemberton, a black teacher at a Wolverhampton school, and involved artists who were children of Caribbean migrants and had been raised in the industrial landscape in and around the West Midlands. As Eddie Chambers, a leading Wolverhampton artist within this movement, argued, given the extent to which Wolverhampton had figured in Powell's speech, the town's art gallery was the perfect setting for their first exhibition 'Black Art an' done'. This was perhaps a confirmation, or maybe a rebuttal, Chambers reflected, of Powell's dire predictions for the town's future as a consequence of its immigrant population.[4] The artists were unapologetically making their presence known in Britain and refusing to ignore the racism surrounding them. The artwork pointed to a new and creative confidence of black people in British society.

Powell's career ended in defeat, yet the last chapter has showed that the politics of Powellism did not die. Returning to Wolverhampton, there are few if any visual traces of Powell remaining. Powell's old constituency house was later rented by a Caribbean family and is now broken up into flats.[5] The newly elected MP in Powell's seat repeatedly claims that the chapter of Powell can now be closed within the city. Yet such hopes do not necessarily correspond to what is currently happening in Wolverhampton where historical debates have resurfaced. At a local level, Powell and his 'Rivers of Blood' speech are well known, and the far right continue to mobilise around the image of blood-filled rivers. A UKIP MEP stated at a meeting in Dudley that multiculturalism would lead to 'rivers of blood', acknowledging afterwards that he had used the image because he had 'wanted to get people's attention' and by using the 'rivers of blood' line he knew people would listen.[6] Most recently, there have been serious attempts to revive Powell, and in early 2018 a public debate was organised by the local newspaper on the legacy of the speech.

Following this debate, the city's Civic and Historical Society announced that an application had been submitted for a blue plaque for Enoch Powell in Wolverhampton and that the proposal would be considered. The local paper took the issue up with fervour, initiating a poll on the question of the plaque, with 13,000 readers responding and with an overall majority supporting the idea. Meanwhile petitions and public letters also responded with determined opposition to the proposal. All three Labour MPs representing the city publicly opposed the idea of a plaque, as did the bishop of Wolverhampton and many trade unionists.[7] The new interest in the plaque, led by the local paper, argued that Powell had good and bad points, but that it was also 'worth remembering that this intelligent and complex man represented Wolverhampton for nearly a quarter of a century'. The newspaper concluded 'there is no doubting Powell's position as a significant figure in the history of Wolverhampton'.[8] The blue plaques secretary for Wolverhampton, Barry Hodgson, explained to the paper: 'My own view is that the plaques should reflect our history, warts and all.'[9] The worry, Hodgson told a different national paper, was that there would be no place in Wolverhampton safe enough for the plaque, with fears that it would be defaced: 'We normally place plaques three metres high, but this would probably have to go four of five metres up' he explained.[10] The newspapers did not clarify that Hodgson was also the UKIP candidate for Wolverhampton South East in the 2017 general election.

This new attempt at Powell's revival in Wolverhampton positions the politician as a curious part of the city's heritage. The plaque of Powell, in these arguments, is simply a cultural attraction for visitors and residents alike to reflect on a completed past. Yet the prophecy of 'Rivers of Blood' is still drawn upon across the country in much more violent ways. Stephen Lawrence's racist suspect murderers were filmed extolling Enoch Powell.[11] Following the riots of 2011 in London and other cities, the Tudor historian David Starkey on national TV explained that he had just been re-reading Enoch Powell and that Powell's prophecy was 'absolutely right in one sense. The Tiber didn't foam with blood but flames lambent. They wrapped around Tottenham and around Clapham'.[12] For Starkey the details of the prophecy did not appear to hold significance, fire replacing blood to predict racial warfare. 'Rivers of Blood' has also been drawn upon as a device not only to predict but, in its very utterance, to turn the vision into a reality. Less than two weeks after Finsbury Park Mosque was targeted in a racist attack and a Muslim man was murdered, the mosque reported that it had since received numerous threatening letters. Mohammed Kozbar, chairman of the Finsbury Park Mosque, said the severity of the threats in the letters had left him concerned that another attack could take place soon. An anonymous letter read: 'There will be rivers of blood flowing down the streets – I will make sure of this.'[13] Powell's calculated words and particularly the insistency of the image of blood-filled rivers has remained a call to arms for implementers of Powell's vision intent on a war between races. Memories of Powell must be contextualised within this more recent history. Rather than a harmless and intriguing historical figure celebrated by a heritage blue plaque in the city, memories of Powell are still drawn by racist supporters to provide direction and a sense of tradition to their action. Powell remains a rallying point for these far right groupings.[14]

For quite understandable reasons then there is also a reluctance to discuss this past at all. For example, when the local newspaper published an article discussing my research on Powell in Wolverhampton, a number of readers expressed a general frustration that the topic of Powell had been returned to at all. One reader wrote to me and said that the response in Wolverhampton to Powell's 'Rivers of Blood' speech had been something of a 'Diana' moment in terms of the obsessive hysteria against Powell's sacking. It was hard to move on from such a moment, much as many of the residents within Wolverhampton tried. Many of these readers insisted that there were nothing fruitful to come of looking back at this bitter history.[15] Behind the calls to ignore Powell, there seemed to be a fear of remembering, a sort of dread, at what a more public history might bring from beneath the surface. In contrast, this book has tried to demonstrate that there was also a rich history of opposition and anti-racism within the area that should be discussed, alongside real fear which had spread within immigrant communities. Both of these intertwined histories are important to recognise if we want to understand racism in Britain today.

There were therfore plans within the city to mark resistance to the 'Rivers of Blood' speech, with 'Wolverhampton Welcomes the World: Many Rivers to Cross' hosting a school play, a rally and a party at the Heritage Centre, once the local Conservative Party HQ. In Birmingham, in the hotel where Powell made his speech, fifty years on, an anti 'Rivers of Blood' event will take place with cultural icons such as the footballer Brendon Bastman due to speak.[16] In planning these events, we had no intention of elevating the speech and the politics of Powell, yet we were aware that on each previous anniversary the debate had been dominated by his supporters. Instead we wanted to organise around a very different politics which celebrated the defeats of Powell, and the hard work of anti-racists.

While mindful of the challenges of publicly discussing this history, it seems all the more important to learn from our past and to note the forceful impact the speech had on those Powell had targeted as well as the resistance that began to emerge.[17] Within public memory we often imagine race and racism within an American history that is well known to us in Britain. When we think of the 'colour bar', for example, we often associate these histories with America. There is a tendency to pull race out from the internal dynamics of Britain, and to repress its much longer history. Racism can often be presented as an aberration which has been injected into British society as an external force. Instead this book has situated the 'Rivers of Blood' speech within a longer history of colonialism and racism within Britain, but also pointed to new ways in which Powell's words were able to reformulate racial ideologies just as decolonisation was spreading across the globe and the post-war boom was gradually coming to an end. For Powell, returning to the local allowed for a new way in which a racialised nation could be imagined, through the imagined voices of 'ordinary' white constituents. The words of Powell, it has been shown, stood at odds with everyday dynamics within the industrial town of Wolverhampton. Yet Powell's speech also had an impact in developing a discourse through which citizens became 'immigrants'. Building on emerging Immigration Acts, Powell was developing a new racial hierarchy that did not rely solely on the old racism of Empire, but extended and reformulated a language of race through targeting the newly formed immigrant enemy. In this sense, the book has provided a closer examination of this discourse through a local study, building on existing literature which has traced these changes on a national scale.[18] This is a living contested history, and fifty years on such struggles have not been resolved. The immigration regime and the 'hostile environment' did not emerge from thin air, but were built on a far longer history of which Powell's intervention played a part. It is hoped that in beginning to remember this past, lessons can be drawn in the current struggles against racism today and any sanitised legacy of Powell can be confronted.

Notes

Introduction

1 J. Enoch Powell, 'Speech to the Annual General Meeting of the West Midlands Area Conservative Political Centre' given in Birmingham, 20 April 1968, in J. Enoch Powell, *Reflections: Selected Writings and Speeches of Enoch Powell* (Bellew, 1992) pp. 161–169.

2 'Powell out of Shadow Cabinet', *The Times*, 22 April 1968.

3 Claimed by the son of the local newspaper editor, Nick Jones, 'Heyday of local press: editor who challenged Enoch Powell on MP's home patch' on his blog www.nicholasjones.org.uk/article-categories/30-media-ethics/general/261-heyday-of-local-press-editor-who-challenged-enoch-powell-on-mps-home-patch (accessed 20 January 2017).

4 Marcus Collins, 'Immigration and opinion polls in postwar Britain', *Modern History Review*, 18.4 (2016): 8–13.

5 Richard Crossman, *Diaries of a Cabinet Minister*, Vol. 3 (Hamish Hamilton and Jonathan Cape, 1977) p. 29.

6 In this sense the book is indebted to the early work of Dr Frank Reeves on histories of race in Wolverhampton. See the archival papers of Dr Frank Reeves, Ref D-DFR, Wolverhampton Archives and his book *Race and Borough Politics* (Gower Publishing Company, 1989).

7 For two substantial biographies of Powell see Robert Shepherd, *Enoch Powell: A Biography* (Pimlico, 1997); Simon Heffer, *Like the Roman: The Life of Enoch Powell* (Weidenfeld & Nicolson, 1998). See also Donley T. Studlar, 'British public opinion, colour issues, and Enoch Powell: a longitudinal analysis', *British Journal of Political Science*, 4.3 (1974): 371–381.

8   Camilla Schofield, *Enoch Powell and the Making of Postcolonial Britain* (Cambridge University Press, 2013).

9   Paul Foot, *The Rise of Enoch Powell* (Penguin Books, 1969).

10   See Satnam Virdee, *Racism, Class and the Racialized Outsider* (Palgrave Macmillan, 2014); Bill Schwarz, ' "The only white man in there": the re-racialisation of England, 1956–1968', *Race & Class*, 38.1 (1996): 65–78.

11   Geoffrey Moorehouse, 'Powell country', *Guardian*, 4 May 1968.

12   'Anger on the hill', *Express and Star*, 1 May 1968.

13   'Dark cloud over race problem', *Express and Star*, 9 May 1968.

14   John Heilpern, 'Town that has lost its reason', *Observer*, 14 July 1968.

15   'Dark question mark', *The Times*, 16 November 1968.

16   *Sunday Times*, 15 June 1969.

17   'Vox Pops on latest Enoch Powell speech', *Midlands News*, ATV, 10 June 1969.

18   Stuart Hall, 'A torpedo aimed at the boiler-room of consensus', *New Statesman*, 17 April 1998.

19   Mike Phillips, 'Enoch Powell: an enigma of awkward passions', *Guardian*, 7 February 2001.

20   Interview with Vanessa Kirkpatrick, email, 15 March 2018.

21   Dick Pixley, *The Closed Question: Race Relations in Britain Today* (Burns & Oates, 1968).

22   No author, *Wolverhampton Memories* (True North Books Limited, 2001); see also Alec Brew, *Wolverhampton: A Century of Change* (Templus Publishing Limited, 2000).

23   Ned Williams, *Wolverhampton: Events, People and Places Over the 20th Century* (Sutton Publishing, 2011).

24   Shepherd, *Enoch Powell*, p. 352.

25   Letter of Karl Marx to A. Vogt in New York, London, 9 April 1870.

26   W. E. B. Du Bois, *Black Reconstruction: An Essay Toward a History of the Part which Black Folk Played in the Attempt to Reconstruct Democracy in America, 1860–1880* (Harcourt, Brace and Company, 1935) p. 700.

27   On this see John Seed, 'Limehouse blues: looking for Chinatown in the London docks, 1900–40', *History Workshop Journal*, 62.1 (2006): 58–85.

28   Charles Critcher, Margaret Parker and Ranjit Sondhi, *Race in the Provincial Press: A Case Study of Five West Midlands Newspapers* (Centre for Contemporary Cultural Studies, University of Birmingham, 1975).

29   An analysis of these letters is given by Amy Whipple, 'Revisiting the "Rivers of Blood" controversy: letters to Enoch Powell', *Journal of British Studies*, 48.3 (2009): 717–735.

30 'Powell rivals march', *Express and Star*, 27 April 1968.

31 *Express and Star*, 10 May 1968.

32 On this relationship see the writings of his family: Rupert Jones, 'My grandparents, Enoch Powell and the day they fell out over his "Rivers of Blood" speech', *Guardian*, 22 October 2016; Jones, 'Heyday of local press'.

33 Editorial, 'Enoch Powell', *Express and Star*, 22 April 1968.

34 Editor, 'Challenge to us all', *Express and Star*, 29 April 1968.

35 For an account of the English working class through the prism of race see Virdee, *Racism, Class and the Racialized Outsider*. On the later anti-racist movement that emerged in 1976 see Roger Huddle and Red Saunders (eds), *Reminiscences of RAR: Rocking Against Racism 1976–1982* (Bookmarks, 2016); Suresh Grover and Jagdish Patel (eds), *Coming of Age: 1976 and the Road to Anti-Racism* (The Monitoring Group, 2017).

1 'The Commonwealth is much too common for me' Another 1968

1 Michael James Roberts and Ryan Moore, 'Peace punks and punks against racism: resource mobilization and frame construction in the punk movement', *Music and Arts in Action*, 2.1 (2009): 21–36.

2 On history of this track see Ian MacDonald, *Revolution in the Head: The Beatles' Records and the Sixties* (Chicago Review Press, 2007).

3 For a global account of 1968 see Tariq Ali and Susan Watkins, *1968: Marching in the Street* (Bloomsbury, 1998); and for a history of this decade that combines the personal with the political see Sheila Rowbotham, *Promise of a Dream: Remembering the Sixties* (Verso, 2001).

4 *Sunday Express*, 4 April 1965, cited in Heffer, *Like the Roman*, p. 376.

5 This 'long calm' is examined by Chris Harman, *The Fire Last Time: 1968 and After* (Bookmarks, 1988).

6 C. A. R. Crosland, 'The transition from capitalism', *New Fabian Essays* (1952): 33–68.

7 C. A. R. Crosland, *The Future of Socialism* (Francis, Ideas, 1956): 177–178.

8 Cited in Heffer, *Like the Roman*, p. 335.

9 Cited in Paul Foot, *Immigration and Race in British Politics* (Penguin Books, 1965) p. 124.

10 Foot, *Immigration and Race in British Politics*.

11 Peter Fryer, *Staying Power: The History of Black People in Britain* (Pluto Press, 1992).

12 Ron Ramdin, *The Making of the Black Working Class in Britain* (Verso Books, 2017).

13 Centre for Contemporary Cultural Studies, *The Empire Strikes Back* (Hutchinson and Co, 1982) p. 30

14 Cited in David Olusoga, *Black and British: A Forgotten History* (Macmillan, 2017) p. 502.

15 The Runnymede Trust and the Radical Statistics Group, *Britain's Black Population* (Heinemann Education Books, 1980).

16 Fryer, *Staying Power*, p. 373.

17 On the discrimination experienced see Ramdin, *The Making of the Black British Working Class*.

18 Enoch Powell, *Express and Star*, 10 October 1964.

19 Stuart Hall, 'Racism and reaction', in *Selected Political Writings: The Great Moving Right Show and Other Essays* (Duke University Press, 2016 [1976]) p. 147.

20 Fryer, *Staying Power*.

21 See Foot, *Immigration and Race in British Politics*.

22 Richard Crossman, *Diaries of a Cabinet Minister*, Vol. 2 (Hamish Hamilton and Jonathan Cape, 1976) p. 679.

23 A. Sivanandan, 'Race, class and the state: the black experience in Britain', *Race and Class*, 17.4 (1976): 354.

24 Foot, *Immigration and Race in British Politics*, p. 235.

25 Harman, *The Fire Last Time*, p. 141.

26 Huw Beynon, *Working for Ford* (EP Publishing, 1976) p. 71.

27 Selina Todd, *The People: The Rise and Fall of the Working Class* (John Murray, 2015) p. 275.

28 See Schofield, *Enoch Powell and the Making of Postcolonial Britain*, pp. 105–114.

29 Cited in Heffer, *Like the Roman*, p. 335.

30 See John Newsinger, *The Blood Never Dried: A People's History of the British Empire* (Bookmarks, 2010) p. 189. For the early response from African Americans to this relationship see Clive Webb, 'Reluctant partners: African Americans and the origins of the special relationship', *Journal of Transatlantic Studies*, 14 (2016): 350–364.

31 'Powellism', *The Times*, 15 July 1965.

32 'Capitalism the best "charity"', *The Times*, 11 December 1964.

33 'Tories in a new world', *The Times*, 28 December 1964.

34 *Sunday Times Magazine*, 29 December 1968.

35 David Widgery, *The Left in Britain 1956–1968* (Penguin Books, 1976) p. 411.

36 On the reinvention of the white race in association with the British working class see Alastair Bonnett, 'How the British working class became white: the symbolic (re)formation of racialized capitalism', *Journal of Historical Sociology*, 11.3 (1998): 316–340.

37 Bill Schwarz, *The White Man's World*, Vol. 1 (Oxford University Press, 2011).

38 Stuart Hall, 'A torpedo aimed at the boiler-room of consensus', *New Statesman*, 17 April 1998.

39 J. Enoch Powell, speech at a public meeting at Carltonle-Willows Grammar School, Gedling, Nottingham, 24 May 1968.

40 J. Enoch Powell, speech at Walsall, 7 February 1968.

41 J. Enoch Powell, speech at a public meeting at Carltonle-Willows Grammar School, Gedling, Nottingham, 24 May 1968.

42 'Dockers and students in angry scenes', *The Times*, 2 May 1968.

43 On this relationship through an examination of James Baldwin see Rob Waters, ' "Britain is no longer white": James Baldwin as a witness to postcolonial Britain', *African American Review*, 46.4 (2013): 715–730.

44 On this history see Graeme Abernethy, ' "Not just an American problem": Malcolm X in Britain', *Atlantic Studies*, 7.3 (2010): 285–307 and Joe Street, 'Malcolm X, Smethwick, and the influence of the African American freedom struggle on British race relations in the 1960s', *Journal of Black Studies*, 38.6 (2008): 932–950.

45 Cited in Street, 'Malcolm X, Smethwick and the influence of the African American freedom struggle on British race relations in the 1960s'.

46 'What the Observer thinks', *Observer*, 14 July 1968.

47 J. Enoch Powell, 'Beyond immigration' interview with Richard Cohen, February 1973, in J. Enoch Powell, *Reflections: Selected Writings and Speeches of Enoch Powell* (Bellew Publishing, 1992) p. 59.

48 Heffer, *Like the Roman*, p. 437.

49 Heffer, *Like the Roman*, pp. 436–437.

50 Schofield, *Enoch Powell and the Making of Postcolonial Britain*.

51 Shepherd, *Enoch Powell*, p. 338.

52 Heffer, *Like the Roman*, p. 441.

53 'BBC apology on "Black Power" ', *The Times*, 23 December 1967.

54 On the emergence of Black Power as a movement in the UK in the period see Robin E. R. Bunce and Paul Field, 'Obi B. Egbuna, CLR James and the birth of Black Power in Britain: black radicalism in Britain 1967–72', *Twentieth Century British History*, 22.3 (2010): 391–414.

55 Powell, 'Speech to the Annual General Meeting of the West Midlands Area Conservative Political Centre', p. 169.

56 On this history of working-class struggle see Ralph Darlington and Dave Lyddon, *Glorious Summer: Class Struggle in Britain, 1972* (Bookmarks, 2001).

2 The world in Wolverhampton

1 Interview with Jarjit Singh Bahra, Wolverhampton, 16 January 2018. Mr Bahra recalls that Mr Powell was a 'nice chap' to speak to as a neighbour, but was completely different when he spoke as a politician.

2 Foot, *The Rise of Enoch Powell*, p. 62.

3 HC Deb, 16 March 1950 vol 472 cols 1315–1319.

4 J. Enoch Powell, 'A letter from your Conservative candidate, Enoch Powell', general election 1951, cited in Heffer, *Like the Roman*, p. 169.

5 Enoch Powell, 'Facing up to Britain's race problem', *Daily Telegraph*, 16 February 1967.

6 Doreen Massey, 'Places and their pasts', *History Workshop Journal*, 39 (1995): 183.

7 Massey, 'Places and their pasts', p. 183. For further studies on the local see Melanie Tebbutt, 'Imagined families and vanished communities: memories of a working class life in Northampton', *History Workshop Journal*, 73 (2012): 144–169; David Featherstone, Anthony Ince, Danny Mackinnon, Kendra Strauss and Andrew Cumbers, 'Progressive localism and the construction of political alternatives', *Transactions of the Institute of British Geographers*, 37.2 (2012): 177–182.

8 For a sociological account which interrogates meanings of everyday racism see Andrew Smith, *Racism and Everyday Life: Social Theory, History and 'Race'* (Springer, 2016).

9 'Speech at the anniversary of the people's paper', Karl Marx, 14 April 1856.

10 Chris Upton, *A History of Wolverhampton* (Phillimore, 1998).

11 There have been heated debates on the Black Country flag and its chains, see 'Black Country flag row: Wolverhampton MP Eleanor Smith defends stance in Commons', *Express and Star*, 19 July 2017.

12 David Bishop, 'Hidden past', BBC Online (2007).

13 'Women slaves of the forge', *Daily Express*, 1 September 1910. Ref: MSS.292C/239.08/3, Warwick Modern Records Centre.

14 Tony Barnsley, *Breaking Their Chains: Mary Macarthur and the Chainmakers' Strike of 1910* (Bookmarks, 2010).

15 Clifford S. Hill, *How Colour Prejudiced is Britain?* (Gollancz, 1965).

16 'Memorandum book of George Molineux', DX-121/24, Wolverhampton Archives. See also Jefny Ashcroft's play on George Africanus, reviewed by the *Express and Star*, 30 July 2016.

17 For histories of the Irish in Wolverhampton see Roger Swift, ' "Another Stafford street row": law, order and the Irish presence in mid-Victorian Wolverhampton', *Immigrants & Minorities*, 3.1 (1984): 5–29; Roger Swift, 'Anti-catholicism and Irish disturbances: public order in mid-Victorian Wolverhampton', *Midland History*, 9.1 (1984): 87–108.

18 Geoffrey Moorehouse, 'Powell country', *Guardian*, 4 May 1968.

19 Brew, *Wolverhampton: A Century of Change*, p. 99.

20 Geoffrey Moorehouse, 'Powell country', *Guardian*, 4 May 1968.

21 Diana Kay and Robert Miles, 'Refugees or migrant workers? The case of the European Volunteer Workers in Britain (1946–1951)', *Journal of Refugee Studies*, 1.3–4 (1988): 214–236.

22 Upton, *A History of Wolverhampton*, p. 130.

23 Interview with Nicholas Ordinans, by email, 26 October 2017.

24 Cited in Upton, *A History of Wolverhampton*, p. 131.

25 BEME Interview with African-Caribbean woman, Interview No. 13 HR, Ref VT-147, Wolverhampton Archives.

26 BEME Interview with Indian male, Interview No. 8 CP, Ref VT-144, Wolverhampton Archives.

27 BEME Interview with Ghanaian man, No. 30 DR, Ref DX-624/6/31, Wolverhampton Archives.

28 BEME Interview with African-Caribbean woman, No. 29 MB, Ref VT-159, Wolverhampton Archives.

29 BEME Interview with African-Caribbean man, No. 12 BB, Ref VT-146, Wolverhampton Archives.

30 'One rule for all races?' *Express and Star*, 5 September 1968.

31 'House refused to coloured man', *The Times*, 12 August 1965.

32 Dilip Hiro, 'The young are ready to hit back', *Observer*, 14 July 1968.

33 Sivanandan, 'Race, class and the state', p. 350.

34 'There is a colour bar and we must face up to it', *Wolverhampton Chronicle*, 18 November 1955.

35 'West Indians want white girls at their dances', *Wolverhampton Chronicle*, 10 May 1957.

36 *Wolverhampton Chronicle*, 3 June 1958.

37 Upton, *A History of Wolverhampton*, p. 130.

38 'We can smash Union says Scala bosses', *Wolverhampton Chronicle*, 20 June 1958.

39 Cited in Ruth Glass, *London's Newcomers: The West Indian Migrants* (Harvard University Press, 1961) pp. 81 and 123.

40 Interview with Avtar Jouhl, Birmingham, 17 January 2017.

41 For a national account of these dance hall colour bars see James Notts, *Going to the Palais: A Social and Cultural History of Dancing and Dance Halls in Britain, 1918–1960* (Oxford University Press, 2015).

42 'Will Jamaicans solve problem of labour shortage?' *Wolverhampton Chronicle*, 23 September 1955.

43 'Will Jamaicans solve problem of labour shortage?' *Wolverhampton Chronicle*, 23 September 1955.

44 John Heilpern, 'Town that has lost its reason', *Observer*, 14 July 1968.

45 'Coloureds not joining the police', *Express and Star*, 22 April 1968.

46 'Pair from "sunshine-land" marry in Wolverhampton', *Wolverhampton Chronicle*, 13 August 1952.

47 'Trapped in mill: worker dies', *Express and Star*, 10 September 1968.

48 John Heilpern, 'Town that has lost its reason', *Observer*, 14 July 1968.

49 John Heilpern, 'Town that has lost its reason', *Observer*, 14 July 1968.

50 John Heilpern, 'Town that has lost its reason', *Observer*, 14 July 1968.

51 Dilip Hiro, 'The young are ready to hit back', *Observer*, 14 July 1968.

52 '44 strikers sacked', *Express and Star*, 23 April 1968.

53 Select Committee on Race Relations and Immigration – minutes of evidence. 31 January 1974. Ref LS/L302/13. Wolverhampton Archives.

54 Interview with Surjit Singh Sandhu, Wolverhampton, 7 February 2018.

55 Interview with Surjit Singh Sandhu, Wolverhampton, 7 February 2018.

56 'Uproar at meeting in Wolverhampton's little Harlem', *Wolverhampton Chronicle*, 21 July 1961.

57 'Coloured labour', *Wolverhampton Chronicle*, 14 September 1956.

58 'Pair from "sunshine-land" marry in Wolverhampton', *Wolverhampton Chronicle*, 13 August 1952

59 'Love is colour blind, say this happy pair', *Wolverhampton Chronicle*, 9 September 1955.

60 'Love is colour blind, say this happy pair', *Wolverhampton Chronicle*, 9 September 1955.

61 BEME Interview with Indian male, Interview No. 8 CP, Ref VT-144, Wolverhampton Archives.

62 Mike Bower, 'Do we risk discrimination against whites?' *Express and Star*, 12 April 1968.

63 Mike Bower, 'Do we risk discrimination against whites?' *Express and Star*, 12 April 1968.

3 Reverberations from 'Rivers of Blood'

1 Theodore W. Allen, *The Invention of the White Race*, Vol. 1 (Verso, 1994).

2 *Express and Star*, 29 April 1968.

3 'Mixed motives of "non racialist" dock marchers', *Guardian*, 24 April 1968.

4 'Dockers march for Powell', *The Times*, 24 April 1968.

5 Cited in Tony Cliff, *A World to Win: Life of a Revolutionary* (Bookmarks, 2000).

6 'Unions, MPs and dockers line up', *Guardian*, 27 April 1968.

7 Chris Harman, 'Workers' unity in the face of Enoch Powell's racism', *Socialist Review*, 324 (2008).

8 John Ezard, 'More go absent for Enoch', *Guardian*, 25 April 1968.

9 Rita Marshall, 'The men who head the marchers', *The Times*, 27 April 1968.

10 'Unions, MPs and dockers line up', *Guardian*, 27 April 1968.

11 Roy Perrot and David Haworth, 'Fears behind white workers' backlash', *Observer*, 28 April 1968.

12 'TUC keeps clear of the Powell question', *Guardian*, 25 April 1968.

13 'Unions, MPs and dockers line up', *Guardian*, 27 April 1968.

14 Roy Perrot and David Haworth, 'Fears behind white workers' backlash', *Observer*, 28 April 1968.

15 'Unions, MPs and dockers line up', *Guardian*, 27 April 1968.

16 Paul Moorman, 'Youth gives answer to Powell', *Morning Star*, 29 April 1968.

17 'Unions, MPs and dockers line up', *Guardian*, 27 April 1968.

18 A. Sivanandan, 'From resistance to rebellion: Asian and Afro-Caribbean struggles in Britain', *Race & Class*, 23.2–3 (1981): 148.

19 'United front faces racists', *Morning Star*, 29 April 1968.

20 Cited in 'Strand and fury', *The Spectator*, 17 January 1969.

21 'Battle of the Strand in South Africa and Rhodesia protest', *The Times*, 13 January 1969.

22 Alan Ross, 'How we took our protest to Powell's headquarters', *Tribune*, 10 May 1968.

23 John Heilpern, 'Town that has lost its reason', *Observer*, 14 July 1968.

24 '50 stop work to back Powell', *The Times*, 23 April 1968.

25 'Back not sack is local cry', *Express and Star*, 24 April 1968.

26 'Support in factories', *Express and Star*, 23 April 1968.

27 'Back not sack is local cry', *Express and Star*, 24 April 1968.

28 'Enoch Powell demonstrations', *Midlands News*, 24 April 1968.

29 *Express and Star*, 26 April 1968.

30 Interview with Mick Powis, 25 October 2017.

31 'Support in factories', *Express and Star*, 23 April 1968.

32 'Dockers in "Powell is right" march', *Express and Star*, 23 April 1968.

33 'Back not sack is local cry', *Express and Star*, 24 April 1968.

34 'Powell: Midlands roundup', *Express and Star*, 3 May 1968.

35 'Hostile but no one hurt', *Express and Star*, 29 April 1968.

36 'Support in factories', *Express and Star*, 23 April 1968.

37 'Hostile but no one hurt', *Express and Star*, 29 April 1968.

38 Sivanandan, 'From resistance to rebellion', p. 112.

39 'Club to vote on colour bar', *Express and Star*, 8 April 1968.

40 'Club doors stay shut to colour', *Express and Star*, 22 April 1968.

41 John Heilpern, 'Town that has lost its reason', *Observer*, 14 July 1968.

42 John Heilpern, 'Town that has lost its reason', *Observer*, 14 July 1968.

43 'Colour bar club threat: I am going to kill you', *Express and Star*, 26 April 1968.

44 Dilip Hiro, 'The young are ready to hit back', *Observer*, 14 July 1968.

45 *Express and Star*, 30 April 1968.

46 *Express and Star*, 30 April 1968.

47 'From calypsos to catcalls', *Express and Star*, 5 August 1968.

48 *Express and Star*, 30 April 1968.

49 Interview with Gurdev Cheema, Wolverhampton, 10 February 2017.

50 Interview with Avtar Jouhl, Birmingham, 17 January 2017.

51 Interview with Anand Chhabra, Wolverhampton, 15 January 2017.

52 Interview with Mrs Jan, Wolverhampton, 7 February 2017.

53 George Barnsby, 'Wolverhampton knows how to deal with its racialists', *Morning Star*, 27 April 1968.

54 George Barnsby, 'Wolverhampton knows how to deal with its racialists', *Morning Star*, 27 April 1968.

55 George Barnsby, 'Wolverhampton knows how to deal with its racialists', *Morning Star*, 27 April 1968.

56 'Bitter attack on Enoch and co', *Express and Star*, 29 April 1968.

57 'Bitter attack on Enoch and co', *Express and Star*, 29 April 1968.

58 George Barnsby, 'Wolverhampton knows how to deal with its racialists', *Morning Star*, 27 April 1968.

59 'An interview with Mr Haynes', *Wolverhampton Chronicle*, 24 April 1968.

60 'Protest petition going to No 10', *The Express and Star*, 22 April 1968.

61 Alan Ross, 'How we took our protest to Powell's headquarters', *Tribune*, 10 May 1968.

62 *Express and Star*, 6 December 1968.

63 'Black-white march', *Socialist Worker*, 1 May 1969.

4 Resistance in the schools and on the buses

1 Powell 'Speech to the Annual General Meeting of the West Midlands Area Conservative Political Centre'.

2 Cited in Heffer, *Like the Roman*, p. 434.

3 BBC Radio, 1967, cited in 'UK Sikhs fight for religious rights', BBC World Service, 2017.

4 David Beetham, *Transport and Turbans: A Comparative Study in Local Politics* (Institute of Race Relations, 1970); Roger Seifert and Andrew Hambler, 'Wearing the turban: the 1967–1969 Sikh bus drivers' dispute in Wolverhampton', *Historical Studies in Industrial Relations*, 37 (2016): 83–111; George Kassimeris and Leonie Jackson, 'Negotiating race and religion in the West Midlands: narratives of inclusion and exclusion during the 1967–69 Wolverhampton bus workers' turban dispute', *Contemporary British History*, 31.3 (2017): 343–365.

5   Select Committee on Race Relations and Immigration – minutes of evidence, 31 January 1974. Ref LS/L302/13. Wolverhampton Archives.

6   'News flashes – West Bromwich bus strike', British Pathe, 3 March 1955.

7   Dhani R. Prem, *The Parliamentary Leper: A History of Colour Prejudice in Britain* (Metric Publications, 1965).

8   'Overtime ban at Wolverhampton: quota of coloured staff disputed', *The Times*, 1 September 1955.

9   'Labour criticism of strikers', *The Times*, 28 February 1955.

10 For a brilliant account of these tensions within the trade union movement in Wolverhampton see Frank Henderson, *Life on the Track: Memoirs of a Socialist Worker* (Trentham Books, 2009).

11 'Love is colour blind, say this happy pair', *Wolverhampton Chronicle*, 9 September 1955.

12 *Wolverhampton Chronicle*, 21 October 1955.

13 Dilip Hiro, 'The young are ready to hit back', *Observer*, 14 July 1968.

14 *Express and Star*, 12 May 1967.

15 Interview with Tarsem Singh Sandhu, Wolverhampton, 14 March 2018.

16 *Express and Star*, 9 August 1967.

17 Interview with Tarsem Singh Sandhu, Wolverhampton, 14 March 2018.

18 *Express and Star*, 9 August 1967.

19 Cited in Beetham, *Transport and Turbans*.

20 *Express and Star*, 9 November 1967.

21 'Silent Sikhs in protest march', *The Times*, 5 February 1968.

22 J. Enoch Powell, speech at Walsall, 7 February 1968.

23 Powell, 'Speech to the Annual General Meeting of the West Midlands Area Conservative Political Centre'.

24 Interview with Jarjit Singh Bahra, Wolverhampton, 16 January 2018.

25 Martin Woollacott, 'Sikh busmen win battle to wear turbans', *Guardian*, 10 April 1969.

26 Arthur Osman, 'Town lifts ban on busmen's turbans', *The Times*, 10 April 1969.

27 Interview with Jarjit Singh Bahra, Wolverhampton, 16 January 2018.

28 Interview with Nicholas Ordinans, email, 26 October 2017.

29 For a longer account of the dispute see Beetham, *Transport and Turbans*.

30 'Tragedy of the lost children', *Wolverhampton Chronicle*, 24 April 1959.

31 'Multi-racial play group a success', *Wolverhampton Chronicle*, 17 April 1968.

32 These tensions are discussed further in Paul Gilroy, *Black Britain: A Photographic History* (Al Saqi, 2007).

33 'G.C.E. has limited value warns Royal School head', *Express and Star*, 17 July 1968.

34 Geoffrey Moorehouse, 'Powell country', *Guardian*, 4 May 1968.

35   The Runnymede Trust and the Radical Statistics Group, *Britain's Black Population*.
36   Cited in Julia McNeal, 'Education', in Steven Abbott (ed.), *The Prevention of Racial Discrimination in Britain* (Oxford University Press, 1971) p. 123.
37   Cited in The Runnymede Trust and the Radical Statistics Group, *Britain's Black Population*.
38   For more on education policy in this period see Sally Tomlinson, *Race and Education: Policy and Politics in Britain* (McGraw-Hill Education, 2008).
39   J. Enoch Powell, speech to London Rotary Club, Eastbourne, 16 November 1968.
40   J. Enoch Powell, speech at Walsall, 7 February 1968.
41   'Crisis in the schools', *Express and Star*, 8 April 1968.
42   'Dark question mark', *The Times*, 16 November 1968.
43   John Heilpern, 'Town that has lost its reason', *Observer*, 14 July 1968.
44   'Immigrant problem "overstated"', *Guardian*, 13 February 1968.
45   Maurice Toaland, 'That 82 per cent school', *Express and Star*, 23 February 1968.
46   Maurice Toaland, 'That 82 per cent school', *Express and Star*, 23 February 1968.
47   George Barnsby, 'Wolverhampton knows how to deal with its racialists', *Morning Star*, 27 April 1968.
48   'Autumn and Spring term report 1967–1968', West Park Primary School personal archival collection.
49   'Immigration and education', *ATV Today*, 20 February 1968.
50   'Spring and Summer term report 1967–1968', West Park Primary School personal archival collection.
51   'West Park School is "happier"', *Express and Star*, 11 June 1968.
52   Interview with Michael Edwards, Manchester, 10 July 2017.
53   'Immigrant children at school in Britain', *Sunday Gleaner*, 21 April 1968. Press cuttings, education folder 27, Ref No: LS/L07CUT/72, Wolverhampton Archives.
54   'Row over "wrong impressions"', *Express and Star*, 4 July 1968.
55   Maurice Toaland, 'That 82 per cent school', *Express and Star*, 23 February 1968.
56   'Autumn and Spring term report 1967–1968', West Park Primary School personal archival collection.
57   Maurice Toaland, 'That 82 per cent school', *Express and Star*, 23 February 1968.
58   'We meet West Midland's first black MP', Channel Four News, 1 November 2017.
59   Angela Spence, 'The girl with snow in her hair and the blue umbrella', *British Future*, forthcoming 2018.
60   John Heilpern, 'Town that has lost its reason', *Observer*, 14 July 1968.
61   Interview with Mrs Jan, Wolverhampton, 7 February 2017.
62   Interview with Patrick Vernon, email, 28 November 2017.
63   '"No child will suffer" says head', *Express and Star*, 4 September 1968.
64   'Instant start to new ideas', *Express and Star*, 5 September 1968.

65 'Migrant only schools a "probability"', *Guardian*, 11 December 1968.

66 'First day at new school', *Express and Star*, 5 September 1968.

67 'First day at new school', *Express and Star*, 5 September 1968.

68 'Choice to be left to children', *Express and Star*, 6 September 1968.

69 J. Enoch Powell, 'Speech to London Rotary Club, Eastbourne', 16 November 1968.

70 'More rows as Grove School is opened', *Express and Star*, 10 December 1968.

71 'Migrant only schools a "probability"', *Guardian*, 11 December 1968.

72 Dilip Hiro, 'The young are ready to hit back', *Observer*, 14 July 1968.

5 A 'monstrous reputation' Remembering Enoch Powell

1 J. Enoch Powell, *Joseph Chamberlain* (Thames & Hudson, 1977) p. 151.

2 Jones, 'Heyday of local press'.

3 'Buses: Strike by bus crews in protest', *ATV Today*, 15 August 1975.

4 Cited in Martin Walker, *The National Front* (Fontana, 1977) p. 110.

5 On this see Richard Thurlow, *Fascism in Britain: A History 1918–1985* (Basil Blackwell, 1987).

6 'Enoch Powell interview', *ATV Today*, 17 April 1973.

7 On this movement see Huddle and Saunders, *Reminiscences of RAR*.

8 'Interview with Margaret Thatcher', *World in Action*, 30 January 1978.

9 Stuart Hall, 'The great moving right show', in *Selected Political Writings*, p. 180.

10 Heffer, *Like the Roman*, p. 847.

11 Heffer, *Like the Roman*, p. 914.

12 Paul Gilroy, 'A land of tea drinking, hokey cokey and rivers of blood', *Guardian*, 18 April 2008.

13 Nigel Hastilow, 'Enoch Powell's legacy much more than one speech: of course he should have a plaque', *Express and Star*, 3 February 2018.

14 Peter Oborne, 'Behind Enoch Powell's monstrous image lay a man of exceptional integrity', *Telegraph*, 13 June 2012.

15 Hall, 'The great moving right show', p. 185.

16 Simon Heffer, 'A prophet yet an outcast: 100 years after his birth, Enoch Powell has been vindicated on a whole host of crucial issues', *Daily Mail*, 15 June 2012.

17 'Enoch Powell Desert Island Discs', BBC Radio 4, 19 February 1989.

18 On this see Michael Kenny, 'Back to the populist future? Understanding nostalgia in contemporary ideological discourse', *Journal of Political Ideologies*, 22.3 (2017): 256–273.

19 Paul Vallely, 'Established values: how the church nearly lost its way over the death of Enoch Powell', *Independent*, 19 February 1998.

20 'Politicians say farewell to Enoch Powell', *BBC News*, 18 February 1998.

21 'Enoch Powell obituary', *Telegraph*, 9 February 1998.

22 'Rivals pay tribute to Enoch Powell', *Independent*, 9 February 1998.

23 'Rivals pay tribute to Enoch Powell', *Independent*, 9 February 1998.

24 'Politicians say farewell to Enoch Powell', *BBC News*, 18 February 1998.

25 Paul Foot, 'Beyond the Powell', *Socialist Review*, March 1998.

26 'Politicians say farewell to Enoch Powell', *BBC News*, 18 February 1998.

27 On this see Gareth Mulvey, 'When policy creates politics: the problematizing of immigration and the consequences for refugee integration in the UK', *Journal of Refugee Studies*, 23.4 (2010): 437–462.

28 Ted Cantle, *Parallel Lives: The Development of Community Cohesion* (Smith Institute, 2008).

29 *The Evening Standard*, 23 October 2006.

30 'Enoch Powell "parallelised" immigration debate', *Telegraph*, 20 April 2008.

31 David Goodhart, 'Too diverse?', *Prospect*, 20 February 2004.

32 'Is this man the left's Enoch Powell?', BBC News Online, 26 April 2004.

33 'White Season', BBC Online, 20 November 2008.

34 Joe Street, 'Shame on the BBC', Institute of Race Relations Website, 11 March 2018.

35 Cited in Joe Street, 'Shame on the BBC', Institute of Race Relations Website, 11 March 2018.

36 'We must be free to speak about the problems of multiculturalism', *Telegraph*, 10 May 2016.

37 'We must be free to speak about the problems of multiculturalism', *Telegraph*, 10 May 2016.

38 'Enoch Powell was not an out-and-out racist', *Telegraph*, 12 November 2010.

39 Daniel Hannan, 'Enoch Powell's monstrous reputation hides the real man', *Telegraph*, 15 December 2014.

40 Nigel Farage speech in Florida on 'Brexit and Trump', 26 November 2016.

41 Nigel Farage, *Fighting Bull* (Biteback, 2010) p. 23.

42 Farage, *Fighting Bull*, p. 74.

43 'Enoch Powell was wrong about immigration', *The Times*, 24 February 2015.

44 'Tory candidate quits over "Powell was right" comments', *Guardian*, 4 November 2007.

45 'Tory councillor apologises for immigration rant', *Coventry Telegraph*, 14 July 2016.

46 *Independent*, 31 January 2017.

47 For a different take on Powell and Brexit see Sally Tomlinson, 'Enoch Powell, empires, immigrants and education', *Race Ethnicity and Education*, 21.1 (2018): 1–14.

48 Zoe Williams, 'Labour can win on immigration: but not by channelling Enoch Powell', *Guardian*, 28 September 2016.

49 Jessica Elgot, 'Some use immigration as euphemism for race, says Diane Abbott', *Guardian*, 21 February 2018.

50 'First Midlands Black MP Eleanor Smith', BBC News Online, 19 June 2017.

51 'Midlands' first black MP wins seat once held by Enoch Powell', *I news*, 10 June 2017.

Conclusion

1 See this dispute led by women reported on in 'Oldbury bus crews', *ATV Today*, 6 May 1974.

2 'Wolverhampton Anti-Racist Material', Ref DFR/6/1, Wolverhampton Archives.

3 'Far too many?' *Panorama*, BBC, 6 February 1978.

4 Eddie Chambers, *Roots & Culture: Cultural Politics in the Making of Black Britain* (IB Tauris, 2016).

5 'Wolverhampton and the shadow of Enoch Powell', *Financial Times*, 4 May 2015.

6 'I've been naive', *Express and Star*, 9 December 2015.

7 Megan Archer, 'Enoch Powell blue plaque: community leaders and politicians sign letter urging plans to be rejected', *Express and Star*, 26 February 2018; Marion Brennan, 'The eyes of the world are on us: Eleanor Smith MP warns against Enoch Powell plaque', *Express and Star*, 12 March 2018.

8 *Express and Star* comment, 'Is Enoch deserving of blue plaque?', *Express and Star*, 30 January 2018.

9 Peter Madeley, 'Blue plaque plan for Enoch Powell in Wolverhampton', *Express and Star*, 30 January 2018.

10 'Enoch Powell blue plaque plan prompts a flurry of threats', *Daily Telegraph*, 3 February 2018.

11 Kathy Marks, 'Lawrence suspects caught on film', *Independent*, 15 June 1998.

12 'David Starkey claims "the whites have become black"', *Guardian*, 13 August 2011.

13 'Finsbury park mosque has been sent threatening letters promising "Rivers of Blood"', *Metro*, 30 June 2017.

14 See British Breitbart website campaigning for Powell plaque, 12 February 2018.

15 'Enoch Powell: did Wolverhampton MP's Rivers of Blood speech create an anti-immigration feeling?' *Express and Star*, 18 October 2017

16 Steven Jones, 'Brendon Batson speaking out at event marking Enoch Powell speech', *Express and Star*, 10 April 2018.

17 For a brilliant earlier history of race and racism on the buses which deals with some of these tensions in public history see Madge Dresser, *Black and White on the Buses: The 1963 Colour Bar Dispute in Bristol* (Bookmarks Publications, 2013).

18 See Rieko Karatani, *Defining British Citizenship: Empire, Commonwealth and Modern Britain* (Frank Cass, 2003); Bridget Anderson, *Us and Them? The Dangerous Politics of Immigration Control* (Oxford University Press, 2013).

Bibliography

Newspapers

Express and Star
Guardian
Independent
Morning Star
Observer
Socialist Worker
Spectator
Sunday Times
Telegraph
The Times
Tribune
Wolverhampton Chronicle

TV

ATV Today
Midlands News
Panorama

Interviews undertaken by author

Jarjit Singh Bahra, Wolverhampton, 16 January 2018. Born in Punjab and first moved to Kenya where he worked for the British army as a technical assistant. Migrated to

Wolverhampton in 1965. Five days after arrival found work as a mechanic and in 1969 after success of the turban dispute he found work on the buses. After a decade he became a shop steward for the union. He worked on the buses for thirty-three years before retirement.

Gurdev Cheema, Wolverhampton, 10 February 2017. Lives in Wolverhampton, migrated from the Punjab and found work on the trains, at the Wolverhampton station ticket machines. He was a leader of the Indian Workers' Association in Wolverhampton.

Anand Chhabra, Wolverhampton, 15 January 2017. Born and lives in Wolverhampton, where his parents migrated from India. Local artist.

Michael Edwards, Manchester, 10 July 2017. Born and grew up in Wolverhampton, where he attended West Park primary school and was the 'white child' in the photographs. Now a lecturer in trade union studies.

Kanchan Jan, Wolverhampton, 7 February 2017. Migrated from India to Wolverhampton and became the second Asian school teacher in the town, after her husband became the first. Now retired.

Avtar Jouhl, Birmingham, 17 January 2017. Leading member of the Indian Workers' Association nationally and trade unionist within the Smethwick foundries.

Vanessa Kirkpatrick, by email, 15 March 2017. Vanessa's parents migrated from the Caribbean to Wolverhampton, although her dad had also worked in America previously. Vanessa was born and grew up in Wolverhampton. She is now a film producer living in Manchester.

Nicholas Ordinans, by email, 26 October 2017. Born and grew up in Wolverhampton, father Jewish refugee from Germany. Nicholas worked on the buses in the late 1960s, and now lives in Australia.

Mick Powis, by email, 25 October 2017. Lives in Wolverhampton, at the time of the speech was a young trade union representative in engineering firm, and later member of the Wolverhampton Anti Racist Committee.

Surjit Singh Sandhu, Wolverhampton, 7 February 2018. Migrated from India to Wolverhampton in 1965 and worked for a decade as a draughtsman and then an engineer designing the machines in a local foundry.

Tarsem Singh Sandhu, Wolverhampton, 14 March 2018. Initiated the turban dispute on Wolverhampton buses when he turned up for work with a grown beard. Now is a businessman in Wolverhampton.

Patrick Vernon, email, 28 November 2017. Born and grew up in Wolverhampton, his parents migrated from Jamaica. He was bussed out of the town in his first year of schooling but then attended Grove primary school. Now a writer and activist in London.

Black and Ethnic Minority Experience (BEME) Wolverhampton interview collection, undertaken 1999–2000.

Interview with African-Caribbean woman, Interview No. 13 HR, Ref VT-147, Wolverhampton Archives.

Interview with Indian male, Interview No. 8 CP, Ref VT-144, Wolverhampton Archives.

Interview with Ghanaian man, No. 30 DR, Ref DX-624/6/31, Wolverhampton Archives.

Interview with African-Caribbean woman, No. 29 MB, Ref VT-159, Wolverhampton Archives.

Interview with African-Caribbean man, No. 12 BB, Ref VT-146, Wolverhampton Archives

Speeches and works of Enoch Powell

Enoch Powell, 'Facing up to Britain's race problem', *Daily Telegraph*, 16 February 1967.

J. Enoch Powell, speech at Walsall, 7 February 1968.

J. Enoch Powell, 'Speech to the Annual General Meeting of the West Midlands Area Conservative Political Centre' given in Birmingham, 20 April 1968, in J. Enoch Powell, *Reflections: Selected Writings and Speeches of Enoch Powell* (Bellew, 1992) pp. 161–169.

J. Enoch Powell, speech at a public meeting at Carltonle-Willows Grammar School, Gedling, Nottingham, 24 May 1968.

J. Enoch Powell, 'Speech to London Rotary Club, Eastbourne', 16 November 1968.

J. Enoch Powell, 'Beyond Immigration' interview with Richard Cohen, February 1973, in J. Enoch Powell, *Reflections: Selected Writings and Speeches of Enoch Powell* (Bellew Publishing, 1992).

'Enoch Powell interview', *ATV Today*, 17 April 1973.

Enoch Powell, *Joseph Chamberlain* (Thames & Hudson, 1977).

Archival material

Papers of Frank Reeves, Ref D-DFR, Wolverhampton Archives.

Education folder 27 – West Park primary school, Ref LS/L07CUT/72, Wolverhampton Archives.

Wolverhampton anti-racist committee papers, Ref D-DFR/6/1, Wolverhampton Archives.

'Strangers in a town', BBC One, 9 December 1969, Ref VT-45, Wolverhampton Archives.

West Park primary school reports of school activities – owned by the school and held on their premises.

Articles and books

Abernethy, Graeme. ' "Not just an American problem": Malcolm X in Britain'. *Atlantic Studies*, 7.3 (2010): 285–307.

Ali, Tariq and Susan Watkins. *1968: Marching in the Street* (Bloomsbury, 1998).

Allen, Theodore W. *The Invention of the White Race*, Vol. 1 (Verso, 1994).

Anderson, Bridget. *Us and Them? The Dangerous Politics of Immigration Control* (Oxford University Press, 2013).

Barnsley, Tony. *Breaking Their Chains: Mary Macarthur and the Chainmakers' Strike of 1910* (Bookmarks, 2010).

Beetham, David. *Transport and Turbans: A Comparative Study in Local Politics* (Institute of Race Relations, 1970).

Beynon, Huw. *Working for Ford* (EP Publishing, 1976).

Bonnett, Alastair. 'How the British working class became white: the symbolic (re) formation of racialized capitalism'. *Journal of Historical Sociology*, 11.3 (1998): 316–340.

Brew, Alec. *Wolverhampton: A Century of Change* (Templus Publishing Limited, 2000).

Bunce, Robin E. R. and Paul Field. 'Obi B. Egbuna, CLR James and the birth of Black Power in Britain: black radicalism in Britain 1967–72'. *Twentieth Century British History*, 22.3 (2010): 391–414.

Cantle, Ted. *Parallel Lives: The Development of Community Cohesion* (Smith Institute, 2008).

Centre for Contemporary Cultural Studies. *The Empire Strikes Back* (Hutchinson and Co, 1982).

Chambers, Eddie. *Roots & Culture: Cultural Politics in the Making of Black Britain* (IB Tauris, 2016).

Chater, Kathleen. 'Job mobility amongst black people in England and Wales during the long eighteenth century'. *Immigrants & Minorities*, 28.2–3 (2010): 113–130.

Cliff, Tony. *A World to Win: Life of a Revolutionary* (Bookmarks, 2000).

Collins, Marcus. 'Immigration and opinion polls in postwar Britain'. *Modern History Review*, 18.4 (2016): 8–13.

Critcher, Charles, Margaret Parker and Ranjit Sondhi, *Race in the Provincial Press: A Case Study of Five West Midlands Newspapers* (Centre for Contemporary Cultural Studies, University of Birmingham, 1975).

Crosland, C. A. R. *The Future of Socialism* (Francis, Ideas, 1956).

Crosland, C. A. R. 'The transition from capitalism'. *New Fabian Essays* (1952): 33–68.

Crossman, Richard. *Diaries of a Cabinet Minister*, Vol. 2 (Hamish Hamilton and Jonathan Cape, 1976).

Crossman, Richard. *Diaries of a Cabinet Minister*, Vol. 3 (Hamish Hamilton and Jonathan Cape, 1977).

Darlington, Ralph and Dave Lyddon. *Glorious Summer: Class Struggle in Britain, 1972* (Bookmarks, 2001).

Dresser, Madge. *Black and White on the Buses: The 1963 Colour Bar Dispute in Bristol* (Bookmarks Publications, 2013).

Du Bois, W. E. B. *Black Reconstruction: An Essay Toward a History of the Part which Black Folk Played in the Attempt to Reconstruct Democracy in America, 1860–1880* (Harcourt, Brace and Company, 1935).

Farage, Nigel. *Fighting Bull* (Biteback, 2010).

Featherstone, David, Anthony Ince, Danny Mackinnon, Kendra Strauss and Andrew Cumbers. 'Progressive localism and the construction of political alternatives'. *Transactions of the Institute of British Geographers*, 37.2 (2012): 177–182.

Foot, Paul. *Immigration and Race in British Politics* (Penguin Books, 1965).

Foot, Paul. *The Rise of Enoch Powell* (Penguin Books, 1969).

Fryer, Peter. *Staying Power: The History of Black People in Britain* (Pluto Press, 1992).

Gilroy, Paul. *Black Britain: A Photographic History* (Al Saqi, 2007).

Glass, Ruth. *London's Newcomers: The West Indian Migrants* (Harvard University Press, 1961).

Grover, Suresh and Jagdish Patel (eds). *Coming of Age: 1976 and the Road to Anti-Racism* (The Monitoring Group, 2017).

Hall, Stuart. *Selected Political Writings: The Great Moving Right Show and Other Essays* (Duke University Press, 2017).

Harman, Chris. *The Fire Last Time: 1968 and After* (Bookmarks, 1988).

Harman, Chris. 'Workers' unity in the face of Enoch Powell's racism', *Socialist Review*, 324 (2008).

Heffer, Simon. *Like the Roman: The Life of Enoch Powell* (Weidenfeld & Nicolson, 1998).

Henderson, Frank. *Life on the Track: Memoirs of a Socialist Worker* (Trentham Books, 2009).

Hill, Clifford S. *How Colour Prejudiced is Britain?* (Gollancz, 1965).

Huddle, Roger and Red Saunders (eds). *Reminiscences of RAR: Rocking Against Racism 1976–1982* (Bookmarks, 2016).

Karatani, Rieko. *Defining British Citizenship: Empire, Commonwealth and Modern Britain* (Frank Cass, 2003).

Kassimeris, George and Leonie Jackson. 'Negotiating race and religion in the West Midlands: narratives of inclusion and exclusion during the 1967–69 Wolverhampton bus workers' turban dispute'. *Contemporary British History*, 31.3 (2017): 343–365.

Kay, Dianna and Robert Miles. 'Refugees or migrant workers? The case of the European Volunteer Workers in Britain (1946–1951)'. *Journal of Refugee Studies*, 1.3–4 (1988): 214–236.

Kenny, Michael. 'Back to the populist future? Understanding nostalgia in contemporary ideological discourse'. *Journal of Political Ideologies*, 22.3 (2017): 256–273.

MacDonald, Ian. *Revolution in the Head: The Beatles' Records and the Sixties* (Chicago Review Press, 2007).

McNeal, Julia. 'Education', in Steven Abbott (ed.), *The Prevention of Racial Discrimination in Britain* (Oxford University Press, 1971).

Massey, Doreen. 'Places and their pasts'. *History Workshop Journal*, 39 (1995): 182–192.

Mulvey, Gareth. 'When policy creates politics: the problematizing of immigration and the consequences for refugee integration in the UK'. *Journal of Refugee Studies*, 23.4 (2010): 437–462.

Newsinger, John. *The Blood Never Dried: A People's History of the British Empire* (Bookmarks, 2010).

No author. *Wolverhampton Memories* (True North Books Limited, 2001).

Notts, James. *Going to the Palais: A Social and Cultural History of Dancing and Dance Halls in Britain, 1918–1960* (Oxford University Press, 2015).

Olusoga, David. *Black and British: A Forgotten History* (Macmillan, 2017).

Pixley, Dick. *The Closed Question: Race Relations in Britain Today* (Burns & Oates, 1968).

Prem, Dhani R. *The Parliamentary Leper: A History of Colour Prejudice in Britain* (Metric Publications, 1965).

Ramdin, Ron. *The Making of the Black Working Class in Britain* (Verso Books, 2017).

Reeves, Frank. *Race and Borough Politics* (Gower Publishing Company, 1989).

Roberts, Michael James and Ryan Moore. 'Peace punks and punks against racism: resource mobilization and frame construction in the punk movement'. *Music and Arts in Action*, 2.1 (2009): 21–36.

Rowbotham, Sheila. *Promise of a Dream: Remembering the Sixties* (Verso, 2001).

The Runnymede Trust and the Radical Statistics Group. *Britain's Black Population* (Heinemann Education Books, 1980).

Schofield, Camilla. *Enoch Powell and the Making of Postcolonial Britain* (Cambridge University Press, 2013).

Schwarz, Bill. ' "The only white man in there": the re-racialisation of England, 1956–1968'. *Race & Class*, 38.1 (1996): 65–78.

Schwarz, Bill. *The White Man's World*, Vol. 1 (Oxford University Press, 2011).

Seed, John. 'Limehouse blues: looking for Chinatown in the London docks, 1900–40'. *History Workshop Journal*, 62.1 (2006): 58–85.

Seifert, Roger and Andrew Hambler. 'Wearing the turban: the 1967–1969 Sikh bus drivers' dispute in Wolverhampton'. *Historical Studies in Industrial Relations*, 37 (2016): 83–111.

Shepherd, Robert. *Enoch Powell: A Biography* (Pimlico, 1997).

Sivanandan, A. 'Race, class and the state: the black experience in Britain'. *Race and Class*, 17.4 (1976): 347–368.

Sivanandan, A. 'From resistance to rebellion: Asian and Afro-Caribbean struggles in Britain'. *Race & Class*, 23.2–3 (1981): 111–152.

Smith, Andrew. *Racism and Everyday Life: Social Theory, History and 'Race'* (Springer, 2016).

Spence, Angela. 'The girl with snow in her hair and the blue umbrella'. *British Future*, (2018) http://www.britishfuture.org/articles/the-girl-with-snow-in-her-hair-and-the-blue-umbrella/ (accessed 30 June 2018).

Street, Joe. 'Malcolm X, Smethwick, and the influence of the African American freedom struggle on British race relations in the 1960s'. *Journal of Black Studies*, 38.6 (2008): 932–950.

Studlar, Donald. 'British public opinion, colour issues, and Enoch Powell: a longitudinal analysis'. *British Journal of Political Science*, 4.3 (1974): 371–381.

Swift, Roger. '"Another Stafford street row": law, order and the Irish presence in mid-Victorian Wolverhampton'. *Immigrants & Minorities*, 3.1 (1984): 5–29.

Swift, Roger. 'Anti-catholicism and Irish disturbances: public order in mid-Victorian Wolverhampton'. *Midland History*, 9.1 (1984): 87–108.

Tebbutt, Melanie. 'Imagined families and vanished communities: memories of a working class life in Northampton'. *History Workshop Journal*, 73 (2012): 144–169.

Thurlow, Richard. *Fascism in Britain: A History 1918–1985* (Basil Blackwell, 1987).

Todd, Selina. *The People: The Rise and Fall of the Working Class* (John Murray, 2015).

Tomlinson, Sally. *Race and Education: Policy and Politics in Britain* (McGraw-Hill Education, 2008).

Tomlinson, Sally. 'Enoch Powell, empires, immigrants and education'. *Race Ethnicity and Education*, 21.1 (2018): 1–14.

Upton, Chris. *A History of Wolverhampton* (Phillimore, 1998).

Virdee, Satnam. *Racism, Class and the Racialized Outsider* (Palgrave Macmillan, 2014).

Walker, Martin. *The National Front* (Fontana, 1977).

Waters, Rob. '"Britain is no longer white": James Baldwin as a witness to postcolonial Britain'. *African American Review*, 46.4 (2013): 715–730.

Webb, Clive. 'Reluctant partners: African Americans and the origins of the special relationship'. *Journal of Transatlantic Studies*, 14 (2016): 350–364.

Whipple, Amy. 'Revisiting the "Rivers of Blood" controversy: letters to Enoch Powell'.
Journal of British Studies, 48.3 (2009): 717–735.

Widgery, David. *The Left in Britain 1956–1968* (Penguin Books, 1976).

Williams, Ned. *Wolverhampton: Events, People and Places Over the 20th Century* (Sutton
Publishing, 2011).

Blogs

Jones, Nick. 'Heyday of local press: editor who challenged Enoch Powell on MP's home
patch' on his blog www.nicholasjones.org.uk/article-categories/30-media-ethics/
general/261-heyday-of-local-press-editor-who-challenged-enoch-powell-on-
mps-home-patch (accessed 20 January 2017).

Index

Abbott, Diane 107
Akali Dal 77
Allen, Rupert 45, 46
America 20, 24, 25, 26, 27, 45, 62, 63, 113

Baird, John 39
BBC 24, 25, 26, 27, 73, 85, 86, 93, 100, 104
Beatles 12, 13
Birmingham Immigration Control
    Association 44
Black Art Movement 109, 110
Black People's Alliance 53
blue plaque 110, 111, 112
BNP *see* British National Party
brewery workers 55, 56
Brexit 103, 105, 106, 108
British National Party (BNP) 101
bus workers 37, 41, 57, 73–79, 92, 109

Carmichael, Stokely 26
Clapton, Eric 12, 93
Crooks, Wade 59, 60
Crossman, Richard 2, 18

dance halls 38, 39
Department of Education and Science
    82, 85, 87
dispersal 82, 83, 85, 88
dockers 23, 50, 51
Dudley 19, 20, 49, 57, 110

Edwards, Bob 62, 63
European Union 93, 105, 108

Farage, Nigel 102–104
foundries 40, 41, 48, 60

Goodhart, David 99, 100
Goodyear Tyre Factory 34, 64, 76
Grove primary school 89, 90
Gupta, Udit Kumar Das 38

Hall, George 58, 59
Hall, Stuart 6, 17, 21, 94
Haynes, Aaron 63
Heath, Edward 20, 72, 92
Hiro, Dilip 75, 90
Hughes, Joe 63

Immigration Acts 17, 18, 19, 113
India 14, 16, 35, 37, 38, 42, 43, 44, 46, 53, 57,
    60, 61, 74, 77, 78, 80, 86
Indian Workers' Association 24, 39, 52, 60
International Socialists 50
Ireland 32, 33, 37, 86, 93
Italy 7, 33, 38, 58, 63, 82, 88

Jamaica 32, 34, 35, 36, 40, 41, 45, 46, 75, 86,
    87, 88, 89, 90, 93
Jan, Mrs 60, 61, 88
Jones, Clement 92

Joshi, Jagmohan 52, 53
Jouhl, Avtar 24, 60

Kenya 18, 26
Keynesianism 20, 94
King, Martin Luther 2, 27, 62

Llewellin-Davies, Eileen 85, 86, 87
London 6, 23, 28, 29, 41, 50, 51, 74, 86, 96, 101, 111
London School of Economics (LSE) 19, 24, 52
LSE *see* London School of Economics

May Day 23

National Front 12, 52, 53, 93
North Wolverhampton Working Men's Club 58, 59

Pakistan 41, 53, 57, 80, 82
Phillips, Trevor 99, 101, 102
Poland 15, 33, 34, 106
police 32, 40, 60, 76

Race Relations Act 47, 48, 55
Rhoden, Ernest 89, 90
Rock against Racism 93, 94, 109

Sandhu, Tarsem Singh 76–79
Saxon, Ruth 58
Scala ballroom 38, 39
Second World War 14, 25, 33, 96
Short, Renee 62

Sikh 29, 73, 75–79
Sivanandan, A. 18, 38, 53, 58
slavery 31, 32
Smethwick 18, 24, 25
Smith, Eleanor 107, 108

Thatcher, Margaret 94, 97
Trade Union Congress 48, 52
Transport and General Workers' Union 55, 74, 75, 77
Transport Committee 73, 75, 77, 79

UKIP 102, 103, 104, 110, 111
Ulster Unionism 93, 94
university students 8, 23, 39, 50, 52, 81, 82

Victoria Sheet Metal Company 57, 64

Walsall 8, 22, 73, 83
West Park primary school 85–88
Williams, Constantine 38
Wolverhampton Anti-Racist Committee 109
Wolverhampton Chamber of Commerce 43, 56
Wolverhampton College of Art and Technology 63, 64
Wolverhampton Communist Party 44, 62
Wolverhampton Council for Racial Harmony 63, 78
Wolverhampton International Friendship League 39

X, Malcolm 24, 25